BRITAIN'S MOTOR BUSES

All that Duple have learned in many years of designing for passenger comfort has gone into this superb interior ... luxury seating with fitted armrests, efficiently sited heating equipment, wide vision windows, paper nets on seat backs, tubular parcel racks with nylon mesh base. Passengers can also listen to the radio, or a commentary on places of interest over the speech amplification equipment.

Probably the most comfortable and reassuring interior ever. This 1959 Super-Vega built by Duple Coachworks on the Bedford SB3 (petrol) and SB1/8 (diesel) chassis seated 41 and was designed for use as a tourer. Cruising at 35-40 mph in its heyday, the vehicle's economy appealed to the owner as did the return bookings gained from passengers attracted by the vistas easily viewed through all the glass.

BRITAIN'S MOTOR BUSES

by

DAVID GLADWIN

BREWIN BOOKS

First published by
K.A.F. Brewin Books, Studley, Warwickshire
1993

ISBN 1 85858 013 7

British Library Cataloguing in Publication Data
A Catalogue record for this book is available from the British Library

Typeset in Baskerville 9pt. and 11pt.
and made and printed in Great Britain
by Supaprint (Redditch)Ltd.

ACKNOWLEDGEMENTS

Where the source of a photograph or of other material is known individual acknowledgements are given at the end of the caption; some remarkable and unique illustrations have resulted from the help given by both commercial interests and fellow enthusiasts. Many photographers have in the past supplied us with beautiful old and new photographs but all too often we do not know their names; but our thanks must go to these men and women. For assistance in the preparation of the text I must express my gratitude to Roger Kidner and his colleagues, an extraordinary amount of help was willingly and freely given. John Carroll of the Crosville Enthusiasts Club researched much data on early Crosville vehicles, and Reg Ludgate of Belfast willingly passes on his encyclopaedic knowldge of local bus and coach operators. In general members of The Omnibus Society have checked data quite uncomplainingly and the staff at Wythall, Long Hanborough and Covent Garden museums have sifted through bits and pieces to find answers. Keith Jenkinson, Editor of Bus Fayre, has given us carte blanche to draw on his excellent productions; Steve Stevens-Stratten of Vintage Roadscene Publications unearthed some little known information on obscure makes. The quotation on p68 is drawn from Mona M. Morgan's "Growing up in Kilvert Country" and is reproduced by permission of the author and the publisher, Gomer Press. My wife continues willingly to type, edit and sort these books and yet still manages to withstand the magnetic charms of elderly coaches and buses. Finally in these hard times I must acknowledge the faith my publisher, Alan Brewin, has in his writers; but he has both a PSV licence and a Certificate of Professional Competence to operate PSVs, and may be biased!

CONTENTS

BOOKS BY THE SAME AUTHOR

English Canals (The Oakwood Press)
Canals of the Welsh Valleys (The Oakwood Press)
Passenger Boats on Inland Waterways (The Oakwood Press)
British Waterways (Spur Books)
The Canals of Britain (B.T. Batsford)
The Waterways of Britain, A Social Panorama (B.T. Batsford)
Victorian & Edwardian Canals (B.T. Batsford)
A Pictorial History of Canals (B.T. Batsford)
Steam on the Road (B.T. Batsford)
Trams on the Road (B.T. Batsford)
Building Britain's Canals (K.A.F. Brewin Books)
Coaching Cavalcade 1910-1970 (K.A.F. Brewin Books)
Midbus, Some Aspects of Midland Bus & Coach Operation (K.A.F. Brewin Books)

WELCOME ABOARD!

The use of the word 'bus' in the title may appear somewhat of a misnomer for half of the photographs in this book show coaches. But the truth is that distinctions were always slightly blurred and of late in order to get high utilization of vehicles the tendancy has been for 'motor omnibuses' to be used in an interchangeable capacity.

If one could use the terms in their 'pure' capacity a bus was a vehicle which plied for hire, stopping and starting at the request of passengers. This held true whether the route was a city one with stops every few hundred yards or a country run where a mile or so might separate a hamlet and the next stop outside Mrs. Jones' farmhouse. The vehicles tended to be rather spartan, with naked bulbs, thinly upholstered seats placed relatively closely together thus restricting leg room, rarely any better than a basic heating system, hard wearing surfaces of rexine and paint, and linoleum or slatted wood floors. It isn't really so long ago that we had a country bus route some 20 miles long where the most reliable vehicles available were a pair of wartime Bedford OWBs complete with wooden seats and no lining to the roof panels which regularly gained an interior layer of frost even when in service. To watch frost spicules slowly creeping across the windscreen both inside and out was an education in bus work!

A coach, though, had (almost invariably) pre-booked seats whether running from Leeds to Blackpool or on a tour of the Wye Valley. When a private hire job was undertaken it was tacitly understood by both parties that a coach, polished and gleaming, would be provided. Had one turned up for a wedding party with a service bus it would not have been favourably received.

Now, anomolous workings are almost commonplace - for example, during one of the railway strikes, a pair of Leyland National buses were used from Birmingham to Glasgow and you cannot get a more basic bus than that, while conversely one local operator (now defunct) used a £160,000 double deck luxury coach as a school bus.

In a perfect world each operator would have a series of vehicles, chosen to reflect the type of work that he or she anticipated carrying out in the forthcoming years. Thus, he or she would have a mini-coach for weddings, a mini-bus for 'special' school work, a 35 seat coach for local excursions where the cost of running a small capacity vehicle could be offset by up-market work and higher prices. Service routes would involve nice new single deckers, and for the local works services a couple of 'cascaded' double-deckers from a well maintained municipal fleet would be fine. Continental work would call for a fast comfortable 'top of the range' machine, but conversely for school bus runs where grafitti and vandalism is the norm a couple of superannuated basic buses would suffice. If, as has occurred, the local council insisted on something better with seatbelts for each child, videos and air suspension (albeit for the same price!) then this work could be dropped and the fleet engineer relieved of the spares and maintenance problems of these old nails.

But it is not a perfect world and each operator at least of secondhand vehicles has where possible, to buy multi-purpose "boaches". And that is where the road passenger carrying vehicle industry all too often shoots itself in its tyres!

Time and time and time again the school bus is indistinguishable from the service bus and the excursion coach and the W.I. outings' coach. Truth to tell they may well be one and the same and this factor is a very real deterrent to would-be passengers. A fair simile is to consider the family car. It bears no resemblance to a London or provincial 'Black Cab'. The 'Black Cab' though is the logical vehicle to buy, efficient, easily maintained, almost indestructable and ageless. But still the motorist buys his Citroen, Peugeot, Rover-Honda, or Ford - anything bar a black cab. So why expect the bus or coach passenger to accept a school bus-type vehicle when they are paying good money for a private hire vehicle?

The chassis and bodywork manufacturers certainly did not build their vehicle to be entirely multi-purpose; the parameters governing the development of a bus (relatively slow speed, strong brakes, ability to withstand continual and varying stresses from both load and road surface) are totally different to that of a coach (ability to cruise 'on the stop' for hours if necessary, soft suspension, fade-free brakes for Alpine work and adequate ventilation) and the drawing office responsible for the bodywork must also take a different approach. The bus body must allow easy and fast entrance and exit of passengers, rugged seating, good illumination, and be built with consideration for the safety of standing passengers. Thus handrails and seat grabs are of vital importance, while flooring must be designed for brutal use (remember stilettos and hob-nailed boots?) and windows should give vision enough to allow passengers both seated and standing to see where they are. And don't forget the bell-pushes or cord!

A coach body on the other hand must be designed to coax people out of their cars for if it cannot do that then the game is lost. Sumptuous seating, a quiet ride, hot drinks machine, toilets, panoramic windows, subdued lighting, video, Musak, are all designed to woo and pamper the passenger. What if the trip to Austria is only an elongated bus journey? The whole ambience must differ from that of a bus to Luton.

One of the saddest facts is that many of the photographs in this book reflect both chassis and body builders who have gone. Some were dragged down by adverse financial circumstances, others failed to evolve their manufacturing methods in the face of new technology.

Seventy years ago, a straight railed, petrol engined chassis was the norm onto which was bolted a wooden framed, plywood panelled or fabric covered body. The frame of the body would almost certain be oak or ash (although Roe used teak, and a few companies softwood) with half lap joints, some degree of bracketry and glue. Onto this was screwed beading, sandwiching the ply skin through a layer of white lead onto the woodwork. Where canvas was used, this called for a technique roughly akin to that of skinning a contemporary aircraft. A propos of this, wire tensioners were not uncommon in a vehicle body of the 1920s and excessive zeal when tightening the adjustable screws could have some interesting effects. Inside coach seats looked, and needed to be, sumptious to compensate for poor springing. Lights were lovely to look at but used as little as possible in the days of dynamos. In any event the drone of the engine, transmission and 'crash' gearbox growls, coupled to the continual bumping and banging of, and in, the bodywork precluded reading. Today is another world! As you step, refreshed, from your steel framed, beautifully well-lit, scientifically seated Plaxton bodied Volvo, after an overnight run from Glasgow, think of Mr. W. Cherrington of Ware, who wrote in June 1929:

"Sir, Some weeks ago I had occasion to travel from Glasgow to London and thought I would try the open road, and booked with the Clan Motorways, of Glasgow. I should like to recommend them to anyone travelling that way.

The vehicle used was a Studebaker saloon coach with nothing elaborate inside but very comfortable seats, and, the main thing in long-distance coaches, plenty of leg room between the seats. The ride takes one through some very interesting country on to Galashiels, where a stop of half an hour is made for lunch. I should like to draw attention here to the restaurant at Galashiels, where, I think, most of the passengers go for refreshment. I had to wait 15 minutes before I could even order anything to eat, which I consider rather bad management. I cannot remember the name of the restaurant, but I certainly think that long-distance coach proprietors should be doing something regarding refreshments en route. To continue, I must compliment the Clan Motorways on the selection of drivers, as I consider them very capable, and efficient, also very punctual, arriving at Newcastle exactly on time, 4.45 p.m.   The second half of my journey was by way of Majestic coaches, leaving Newcastle at 8 p.m. and arriving in London at 7 a.m. on the following morning. I would not recommend night travel personally, as I suffered from dizziness in the eyes for a day or two afterwards, but here again I must compliment Mr. Armstrong, of Ebchester, on his selection of both coaches and drivers.   Bodies by Duple, of Hendon, mounted on Gilford chassis.   W. Cherrington".

On a personal note, one aspect of motor omnibus operations today that bothers me is the proliferation of mini-buses zooming around bus stations.   Am I alone in finding a dislike of their rasping engines, squealing brakes, and often gaudy colours?   I am aware that many elderly would-be passengers find their rapid and seemingly erratic movements quite intimidating and indeed a percentage of mini-bus drivers do show aggressive tendencies towards other road users, whether pedestrians or on wheels, and within the confines of an enclosed area this hostility seems to be exacerbated.   Perhaps the change to midi-buses will calm the atmosphere again, and help to take would-be passengers from their cars.   The other side of the coin is to be found in the ranks of many bus and coach operators, small and large, whose drivers and couriers really welcome passengers and appear to enjoy their work - these are the men and women Mr. Cherrington would feel at home with.

During the 1920s and to a lesser extent 1930s picture postcards were sold by the million and almost all were of extremely high quality.   There is no clue who published this, although it was posted 2 July 1930 from "London W1" to Toronto, Canada and has subsequently found its way back.

Ludgate Circus was built between 1864 and 1875 at the junction of Ludgate Hill and Fleet Street.   The viaduct across Ludgate Hill (visible on the left) was built for the extension of the London, Chatham & Dover Railway 'City Line' from Blackfriars to Farringdon Street (Met Rly) and opened to traffic on 1 Jan 1865 and closed 3 March 1929.   The lines across the viaduct led after 1874 also to Holborn Viaduct station; from 1866 via the Snow Hill tunnel to a junction near Farringdon St with the Metropolitan Railway 'Widened Lines'.   Traffic across it included the LCDR service to Farringdon Street and from 1871 also to Moorgate St., LCDR trains to the Great Northern Railway stations and vice versa, the South Eastern Railway service from Woolwich Arsenal station to various GNR stations, and GNR reciprocal trains.   Until the early thirties all freight trains to Hither Green sorting sidings went that way.   Holborn Viaduct station closed 26 January 1990 and the bridge was dismantled that year.

The first of the "K" class buses which seated 46 and were 7' 2" wide (2.2m) entered service 26 August 1919, with an AEC chassis, 28 h.p. petrol engine and a Walthamstow built body.   K266 (on the right) built in 1920 as one of 1132 in the class was really then most modern this being the first design of London bus to seat the driver alongside the engine.

On the left, showing its shapely rear, is a member of the "S" class in the S98-177 series.   This was a successor design to the "K" as following an increase in the permitted weight during 1920, a larger engine of 35 h.p. and increased capacity to 54 seats became possible.   Including single-deckers, 928 "S" type were built.   ➤

S 15368   LUDGATE CIRCUS, LONDON, E.C.4   30

Lincoln Bus Station, the Interior   PN1051

This postcard of Lincoln Bus Station shows that in the 1950s there was still a pride in showing aspects of bus and coach operation. The vehicles are a typical mixture of various Bristol types, with the only one loading destined for Brigg. The waiting room looks quite inviting, and the parcels and left luggage office is manned. Immediately in the right hand foreground is a milk dispensing machine - very much a period piece. In today's deregulated age no one operator is able to undertake works of this kind and generally councils are unwilling or unable to offer sufficient funds, resulting in today's termini often being found under multi-storey car-parks, office blocks or shopping malls.

The card was issued by the Lincolnshire Road Car Company Limited who offered "Local bus services - Express coach services - coach cruising holidays - Coaches and buses for hire - Day tours and excursions" and bearing in mind the poor incomes in Lincolnshire did it all rather well.

Three levels were in use at Paul Street Coach & Bus Station, Exeter, when this photograph was taken. At the top level can be seen service buses of Devon General and Exeter Corporation, in the middle can just be discerned the figure of a baggage handler standing on the roof of a long-haul Royal Blue service coach, and below are mostly vehicles of Greenslades, the Exeter based operator, plus others of unknown owners. The nearest coach is a Leyland half-cab with rather outdated 'broken back' styled bodywork, and behind this are a number of Bedford OBs, plus an early Commer, with Duple bodies. The second tranche are mostly Bedford OBs with varying bodywork but the two with sun-visors to the rear look like 26-seat pre-war Duple bodies mounted on 1937/8 Bedford chassis. The opening roofs are of interest, some being all canvas, others having rigid sliding sections, but all allow a degree of ventilation we can no longer enjoy today. The cars are another matter with at least a dozen makes visible.

This Beadle-Commer is altogether rather an unusual example of British coach building, differing from orthodox vehicles in three ways. Firstly, there was no true chassis, John C. Beadle Ltd., of Dartford, Kent, rather specializing in using what might be called a monocoque structure onto which was hung the mechanical components. The choice of mechanics for this 'Rochester' model fell upon Commer who were never even remotely among the big players in the bus builders league and to cap it all Beadle chose to use the Commer TS3 two stroke 3-cylinder diesel engine in which each cylinder contained two opposed pistons working a common crankshaft, itself located beneath the combustion area. As was normal for a two-stroke fuel was forced through ports, rather than drawn past valves and the blower's distinctive throaty roar marked the passing of a TS3 engine for many a year. Yorkshire Woollen District (a British Electric Traction Group company) purchased a dozen of this model in 1957 (CHD 359-370) and one is seen when almost brand new.

In Coach and Bus Week, November 14 1992, Trevor Jones, the Marketing Manager of the Lewisham, London based operator Selkent, wrote that they valued the support they received from enthusiasts very highly indeed but added a caveat that they were not amused when these 'enthusiasts' arrived to visit the garage by car!

The Omnibus Society members would not dream of doing such a thing and indeed part of the pleasure lies in the ride which is enjoyed in good company. One such visit in mid-1992 led to an unusually animated scene inside the yard of Chester City Transport.

The vehicles are somewhat less than common, having Dennis Dominator chassis with Northern Counties (YMA 100W, HMA 104X) and East Lancs (A106 KRN, DBV2/4W bodywork. And to cap it all underneath the noses of the buses on the left can be discerned 3' 6'' tramtrack - a relic of a system which closed on 15 December, 1935.

George Patterson & Sons of Beadnell, Northumberland, have probably some of the worst conditions imaginable to operate in. Only 20 miles (32 km) from Berwick-upon-Tweed and almost opposite the Farne Islands the weather can wreak havoc on the roads, with loose sand blown over everywhere in summer, and frozen sea spray in winter. It says much for their staff that Pattersons coaches always appear to be well maintained and a good advertisement for local coaching. Plaxton bodywork is favoured on lightweight chassis, and their depot was photographed in 1990.

The garages, depots and booking offices of bus and coach operators often reflect the type of work they do, and, at a quiet time many have on show some less-than-usual vehicles. The tendency nowadays is for old-established companies to either sell off, or after take-over, to have sold off their prime assets: the town or city centre garage. This will be replaced (usually on lease) by a shed-type building on an anonymous industrial site. The days when a good coach company had a prestigious property in town and a booking agent in virtually every village are gone. Any bus company worth its salt always stabled vehicles in useful locations to reduce 'dead' mileage. Typically Midland Red had two rather attractive garages (one single deck and the other for 'staircase vehicles') strategically placed in Leamington; now they have a rather ugly tin-can building near the station. This is the premises of Wrights of Brandon, Norfolk. The signboard reads: "Travel the Wright way. Mini-Midi-Maxi Coach Hire". and gives the telephone number. In front of the house is a Volkswagen mini-bus.

A small part of the fleet run by Howard's Tours, (Whitby), of the White Point Garage, Whitby, North Yorkshire is shown here, sometime in the late 1960s. The left hand vehicle (DWP 326B) is a well maintained Bedford/Plaxton and that on the right (OHG 325) has a typically Duple front, but the one in the middle is quite a rarity, insofar as it has a Commer/Karrier 32A chassis, powered by a 2267 c.c. Humber Hawk petrol engine and a rather elegant Reading Coachworks of Portsmouth 14 seat body. Registered 956 CLF she would have been quite fast, cruising at 50-55 mph, economic (15-20 mpg) but, like many Reading bodies have suffered from structural weaknesses after a decade or so. But a pretty little machine, none-the-less.

Busways Travel Services Limited is a private limited company established by the Transport Act, 1985 to acquire the bus undertaking of Tyne and Wear Passenger Transport Executive. Busways commenced trading on 26 October, 1986. Busways predecessors were the municipal undertakings in Newcastle upon Tyne, South Shields and Sunderland and also private companies acquired in 1973 and 1975. On Friday 5 May 1989 the employees of the company successfully completed their buyout and now all the shares in the company are held by the management and employees under an Employee Share Owner-ship Plan (ESOP). This photograph was taken during 1990 and shows left to right, G921 TCU, a 1989 Scania with 51 seat Alexander body, C604 LFT, 1986 Leyland Olympian, again with an Alexander body but seating 76, and SCN 256S, an elderly (1977) Leyland Atlantean whose 'traditional' Alexander body seats 86. All were enhanced by a vinyl sticker stating the company was employee owned.

30 March 1992 and Yarranton Brothers of Eardiston's C21 KBM, a Plaxton bodied 1986 Bedford YNV, once a demonstrator for Bedford Motors, turns into Worcester bus station, her gleaming paintwork reflected in the Spring puddles. Behind is C347 PNP, a Midland Red West Mercedes L608D, with Robin Hood 20-seat body conversion on the 144 Droitwich-Worcester run.

The York... Traffic Area
Hillcrest H...
386 Harehills L...e
Leeds LS9 6NF

Road Traffic Act 1960

CERTIFICATE No.   **B 78842**

Certificate of Fitness

I, the undersigned, a CERTIFYING OFFICER duly appointed by the Secretary of State for Transport hereby certify, in accordance with the provisions of the Road Traffic Act 1960, that the vehicle described below fulfils the prescribed conditions as to the

fitness in respect of its use as a....STAGE.........carriage.

DESCRIPTION OF VEHICLE

Chassis No..KY..607844..   Registration Mark
(See Note below)   **R NE 693 W**

Make and Model..BEDFORD. CF 350.........

Year of Manufacture of Chassis or first registration.......1980.......

Seating { Upper Deck...—.........
{ Lower Deck....17......

Type of Body...S.D. SALOON.......

This certificate shall continue in force until..22 July 1987.....

Fee £25 £35

Date of issue..23. 7. 80.......   ....
Certifying Officer

Notes

1. If the vehicle does not appear to have been registered under the Vehicles (Excise) Act, 1971, that fact will be indicated. In such case the holder of this certificate is required to notify the registration mark of the vehicle to the Traffic Commissioners immediately after it has been assigned and to send or deliver this certificate to them for endorsement accordingly.

2. If any alteration, otherwise than by way of replacement of parts, is made to the structure or fixed equipment of the vehicle to which this certificate relates, the holder of the public service vehicle licence is required to give notice of the alteration to the Traffic Commissioners for the Traffic Area in which the licence was issued.

PSV 4

Department of Transport
ROAD TRAFFIC ACT 1972, Section 43

Public Service Vehicle
Test Certificate

Serial Number

626636 A

The public service vehicle of which the registration mark * is   **R NE 693 W**.

having been examined under section 43 of the Road Traffic Act 1972 and in accordance with the regulations and directions issued under that section, it is hereby certified that the vehicle was found to comply with the prescribed requirements.

* When no registration mark is exhibited on the vehicle, the chassis or serial number should be shown.

Make   **BEDFORD.**

Date of issue **September 27th 1990** Approximate year of manufacture   **1980.**

Date of expiry **September 26th 1991. NINETY ONE**

Serial Number of immediately preceding Test Certificate   **N A ,**   Signature of Inspector/Tester

(To be entered when the above date of expiry is more than 12 months after the above date of issue.)

Authentication Stamp

WARNING

**Certificates showing
alterations should
not be issued or
accepted**

(See Notes overleaf)

VTP 20 (April 87)

TECHNICAL DIGRESSION

Every new Public Service Vehicls (PSV) or, as now, Passenger Carrying Vehicle (PCV) with more than eight seats that enters revenue earning service must have a Certificate of Initial Fitness. Broadly this certifies that the vehicle has been tested and is suitable for use as a PCV.

At one time this C.I.F. gave the operator a clear seven year period in which the vehicle could earn its keep, but at the end of the seven years re-certification was required which, in effect, often meant a total rebuild. Two results came from this. Many PSVs were designed for a seven year life, and there was a fair old trade in forged certificates to enable a none too scrupulous or penurious operator to keep his 'summer only' vehicles on the road. One might add that very often towards the end of the seven years some vehicles (those having no money spent on them) were 'interesting' to drive. But now all PCVs must be tested each year at the anniversary of their registration. A full PCV will require a Class VI certificate, as shown here, a preserved, Community or LEA school bus, the much less complicated Class V and a PSV with less than eight seats the ordinary car-type test. Whether it is right that an Education Authority vehicle should have a lesser test than a private operator's bus on the same work is a matter of debate, but fortunately all vehicles on the road can, given cause, be tested by authorized police officers and Department of Transport examiners.

During the history of passenger carrying vehicles certain engineering and social changes have altered the course of the industry.

A typical example is the Leyland Titan chassis which changed the double deck vehicle from a high ungainly lumbering vehicle to one that was far lower and therefore inherently safer. A social change was the implementation of the 1930 Road Traffic Act which, in one stroke, regulated the industry almost entirely in favour of the big companies with hundreds if not thousands of small firms ceasing to trade. On the technical side, self-starters and anti-freeze compounds made a driver's job so much better as later did power steering and synchromesh gearboxes, while the first use of pneumatic tyres on double deck buses (Wolverhampton, 1927) vastly improved the passengers conditions of travel.

Two other changes are summed up in this cartoon. The caption reads "There is no need for drivers to warm their engines up - diesel-engined buses can be driven away cold in the most icy weather". But this sketch, dating back to 1957 also foresaw that blackest of days when, for economy, the conductor ceased to be necessary. In that one occurrence the whole face of public *service* changed; no longer could the conductor help the old lady on, or the mother with her pram, or call out a stop for some lost soul. Conductors handled parcels and drunks, chaffed the girls and consoled the lonely, kept an eye on safety and quelled vandalism before it took a hold. From engine in front, stairs at the back and two staff, now its engine in the back, stairs in the front and one lonely soul, poorly enough paid, trying to be all things to all people.

There is no need for drivers to warm their engines up—diesel-engined buses can be driven away cold even in the most icy weather.

KH 5239 was, in many ways, already an anachronism when delivered in 1928, for a year earlier the first new-design Leyland Titan TDI had left the works - a vehicle which in the design not only of the body (and that was advanced enough) but also in its low-height chassis made all other double-deckers immediately out-of-date.

The model shown, the Bristol A-type, was first made available in 1925 and in its three year life only twenty-three chassis were built; 18 becoming double-deckers, 4 single deckers and the longest lived, a horsebox.

Powered (if that is the word) by a particularly feeble four-cylinder petrol engine type 'FW' of a nominal 36 h.p., KH 5239 had a 50-seat Roe body and as shown here was new to Hull Corporation.

C138 YJT, seen here at Leicester in August 1992 is one of only 173 Metroliners ever built and of those 130 were double deckers. Of this particular model (albeit there were specification variations batch to batch) just 127 were assembled at Saltley, but they have been described as 'hugely successful' and 'the ultimate coach'. Sales of only 137 Guy Wulfrunians led to the takeover of Guy by Jaguar, and in 1989, shortly after delivering the last of an updated version, MCW in turn closed their doors.

The first double-deck Metroliner appeared on show in 1982, and was fitted with a Cummins L10 engine, and fully automatic Voith gearbox with integral retarder. With hindsight we can see that the Achilles Heel of the Metroliner lay in the manufacturers use of a separate chassis and beam front axle which combined to ensure an overall height of 4.23m (13' 10½''). This limited sales to the UK, as a vehicle commonly used on the Continent must not exceed 4m (13' 1½''). Those 9'' doomed Metroliner sales.

Two variants were purchased - the Rapide, with 73 reclining seats, dual doors with centre staircase, toilet, vending machine and curtains, and the more basic Express, single entrance/exit, 84 seats and no 'luxury' fittings. Completed vehicles totalled 68 and 59 respectively. Although still young vehicles a number have already been scrapped due to lack of spares and this particular machine had some corrosion visible here and there in the panelling. But the ride was superlative and it is a shame the Metroliner is another British might-have-been.

A BRITISH TRIUMPH.

WE MAKE

MOTOR OMNIBUSES.
MOTOR CHARABANCS.
MOTOR VANS.
MOTOR WAGONS.
MOTOR LAUNCHES.

"The Omnibus de Luxe."

THE

SCOTT-STIRLING

ACCELERATED DELIVERY.

Owing to the rapid execution of our Works Extensions, we are now booking Orders for Early Delivery.

THE

SCOTT-STIRLING

"The Omnibus de Luxe."

"The Official Inspection and Trial of the New Scott-Stirling Double-deck Omnibuses for the London Power Omnibus Co took place last Saturday. . . . A most conspicuous feature was its **Smooth and Silent Running.**"

SCOTT,
STIRLING
and CO., Ltd.,
Twickenham,
LONDON.

To meet the enormous demand which has arisen for the "Scott-Stirling" Commercial Motors, we will shortly make our

24 h.p. Omnibus for Thirty-four Passengers.

OUTPUT 500 OMNIBUSES

PER ANNUM.

This magnificent advertisement measuring 'on the hoof' 12" x 18" and taken from Motor Traction April 1906, rather belies the fact that Scott-Stirling went out of business a year later.   The 'Pioneer' was the fleet name of one of the thirty or so companies that emerged during the early days of London motor bus operation.   The London Power Omnibus Company Limited began in 1902, as the London Motor Omnibus Syndicate running rather unsuccessful single deck Scott-Stirling buses between Cricklewood and Oxford Circus.   In 1905 a fleet of double-deck variants buses were ordered by the Managing Director, a Mr. John Stirling.   As can be seen from both the advertisement and the photograph these were curious looking machines, seating 16 inside, 18 on top and two alongside the driver.   Interestingly though they had electric lighting, powered by a battery or accumulator which was recharged overnight at the Pioneer garage, Langdon Road, Cricklewood.   They also experimented with different hub and wheel arrangements, No.14 on the right of the advertisement has Robson wheels, having steel hubs and felloes, which may have been fitted with the patented Glyda hubs used on some models.   The inordinate length of the rear hubs in the photograph are of interest;   they probably acted as reservoirs for grease or heavy oil, certainly they were liable to damage pedestrians legs.   By 1907 there were 63 Scott-Stirling buses in service, but the Power company were plagued by disputes over delivery notwithstanding the works having been extended the previous year.   1906-7 only 40 were built in the year making a mockery of the advertisements which promised 500.

Both manufacturers and operators were gone by the end of 1907.

R.W. Kidner Collection

Sometime during the first world war, probably late 1914, these B class buses were photographed at Grove Park, Lee, London.   We are told this was in use as an Army (not then Royal) Service Corps Collecting depot.   "It looks very casual; the corporal does not seem to have saluted the officer just passing him . . .".

The first B-class buses to be 'called-up', were new single deckers withdrawn from service on 1 August 1914, and fitted out for ambulance duties.   War commenced on 4 August.   Grove Park was an ASC storage depot and out of the 954 B-types requisitioned, many were fitted with lorry bodies as either mobile wireless equipment 'controls', ration wagons or lofts for carrier pigeons.   But the B-type as a bus excelled itself carrying (officially) 24 fully equipped men at a booked average speed of either 10 (in convoy) or 12 (individual vehicles) m.p.h.   Their endurance was phenomenal and after return to the UK many were to re-enter service.   One diary records "I left Grove Park on 22 October 1914 with the very same bus (B1219) as I had been on service with, on the 67 route, Raynes Park to Liverpool Street".   The bus and her driver went to Ypres, La Bassee, Neuve Chapelle, Loos and Messines Ridge among her other wanderings.   After the war B1219 was purchased back from the War Department and re-entered service.

The "B" type body resulted to a very great extent from restrictions laid down by the London Commissioner of Police in 1909. A survey showed that too many vehicles were making excessive noise (both from the transmission and the tyres upon cobbles) too much smoke (Clarksons steamers were singled out as a cause of complaint with their occasional paraffin 'flash backs') and too much weight. Speed was already limited to 20 m.p.h., width at 7'2", but unladen weight was reduced to 3½ tons, laden to 6.

The first B types entered service on 18 October 1910, normally powered by a 28 h.p. 4-cylinder engine having a 3-speed + reverse gearbox and a wormdrive back axle (7.33:1 ratio). The chassis was a true 'composite' of ash, reinforced with steel flitch plates, but the foot brakes worked only on the rear wheels via internally expanding shoes operating in a drum. The handbrake (like early Land Rovers) was only for parking and gripped the driving shaft. 2900 B-type buses were built, albeit with many variations on the basic theme, the last remaining in service until 12 October 1926.

East Surrey 63 was a true 'B' type, body number 694 being built in an AEC 'YC' (War Department) chassis. The 16-spoke cast wheels were favoured for these chassis and were also used by Straker for their designs. 63 was in service with East Surrey from 13 April 1922 until 1st April 1926.

G. Robbins Collection

21

On 17 December 1930 No. 60 within the Belfast Corporation bus fleet was delivered. The chassis was a Leyland TD1, serial number 71615 and the body, a full height 52 seater, was built by Eastwood & Kenning. Registered AZ 6439 No. 60 was one of a batch of six, all of whom had their bodywork rebuilt by Harkness, the local bodybuilders in 1940, although this only postponed their needing new bodies in 1943. After a twenty year chassis life, all were withdrawn in 1950 and presumably scrapped. Just over 14' in height, with a total weight of under 6 tons, the unique part of these vehicles lay in that their chassis layout was the first to be cranked between the axles, to give a low level entrance and floor combined with adequate headroom in the saloon. The original engines were of 6.8 litre capacity developing 90 h.p. at 2000 r.p.m., a design that, heavily modified, in diesel form remained in production until 1948.

R.C. Ludgate Collection

RV 72.

Bolton Corporation Tramways took delivery of this Leyland TD1 in 1929. The TD1 first appeared on show at the 1927 Olympia (London) Commercial & Motor Show and orders came in such great numbers that Leyland Motors were unable to produce bodies fast enough to equal the demand. 13' (3.96m) high the lowbridge model was at least 2' (60cm) lower than its rivals, giving greater versatility in route working. Around 2400 were built in the four years the chassis was available, with the lowbridge type being standard although a 14' (4.26m) highbridge model was available from 1930 seating 51 or 52 rather than the 48 of WL 3302. Enclosed or open staircase could be chosen from 1929, and open or closed top-decks were another option.

The PSV (Conditions of Fitness Equipment Use and Certification) Regulations 1981 to a considerable extent merely re-confirmed many existing regulations. Not the least of these was and is a requirement that all new vehicles have to be tilt-tested. Simply, the PSVs must not overturn before the table on which it stands has reached in the case of fully laden single deckers 35°, and in the case of double deckers with the upstairs only fully laden 28°. Both angles presume the deck or table to be horizontal. Obviously live people are not used but weights equal to 140 lbs. (63.5 kg) per passenger plus driver (and conductor/courier where relevant). It is of note that a surprising number of Continental vehicles fail this test when first offered and usually require modification to the suspension before passing.

This tilt test took place in May 1932 at the Chiswick Works of the London General Omnibus Company. JG 2602 had a Morris Commercial Imperial chassis, No. 005, with a Park Royal low height 55 seat body, which was subsequently delivered to the East Kent Road Car Company in June 1932. She was numerically the second, but the first to be put into service, JG 2601 being held back for slight modification and not being delivered until July with the rest of the batch of 15. A further ten arrived around the end of the year. The demonstrator had already been obtained in January but no further Imperials followed and in the event only 83 were manufactured. A shortage of spares coupled to very short lived engines meant the first withdrawal from the East Kent fleet came in 1938, the bulk being scrapped in March 1939.

The M & D and East Kent Bus Club

POWER UNIT MOUNTING AND REMOVAL - The patented power unit mounting arrangement, incorporated on this vehicle, constitutes the most practical solution of the engine removal problem, as may be understood from the following brief description.

The front of the power unit is supported in a trunnion bearing carried on the frame front cross tube, which cross member is mounted in the two front dumb-irons and also carries the radiator. Two arms, cast on the flywheel casing, carry spherical seatings which are secured by spring loaded bolts to seats integral with the rear shackle brackets of the front springs, and so support the rear of the power unit. This three-point suspension system, incorporating a trunnion bearing for the front and spherical seatings for the rear, ensures that the engine is practically immune from distortional stress, irrespective of frame movement.

Removal - It will be understood from the foregoing that the power unit is, in effect, mounted on the four special front spring anchor brackets; these brackets are held to the frame by large rustproofed set bolts passing into suitable inside blocks and thus the principle provides for the ready removal of the complete power unit and mounting. After disconnecting exhaust pipe, fuel pipe, etc., and the various controls, the spring anchor bracket set bolts are withdrawn, the main frame is jacked up each side, a simple tail skid (supplied with tool kit) is affixed to the gearbox, and the whole unit is then free to be rolled out to a convenient point and, if necessary, lifted from the axle.

Using the front axle and tail skid as a carriage, in the manner described, **a complete power unit change may be effected in a minimum of time** should the occasion arise, and the vehicle quickly placed back in service.

On the face of it, this is a perfectly normal double-deck bus. ("Provincial") fleet was an example of British bus-building ingenuity. London Transport and nigh on impossible for relatively small companies. But in reality No. 14 in the Gosport and Fareham During the war obtaining new buses was difficult for

The chassis of EOR 251 began life in 1932 as a normal control (bonneted) AEC Mandator with an oil tanker body. In 1944 this was rebuilt by the company to forward control, fitted with an AEC 7.7 litre diesel engine, bus radiator, and a dropped rear frame for the entrance.

The body was only the second 'utility' built by the firm of Reading & Co., Coachbuilders, Portsmouth and seated 56.

This ensemble was withdrawn in 1960 when the chassis was 28 years old and the body 16. But the latter, tidied up, was refitted to a 1947 chassis, serving to carry passengers into its 20th year.

L 82

THE CENOTAPH AND WHITEHALL

During World War II manufacture of munitions and service vehicles had to take priority, but the lack of new vehicles put an enormous strain on the existing PSV services. Add to this a shortage of maintenance personnel, greatly increased passenger loads and the results of enemy action and it became obvious that chassis in excess of those being made by Guy Motors were vital. In 1943 Daimler re-started production of a new vehicle type, the CWG 6 (Commercial, War, Gardner engine) of which 100 were built before the AEC 7.7 litre engined CWA 6 chassis, became the normally available model. Fortunately for drivers, the Daimler pre-selective gearbox and fluid flywheel were still used. Between 1944 and 1946 281 of this model were delivered to London Transport and in this photograph the nearest bus, D28 in the LT fleet (GLX 914), entered service with a Duple 56 seat utility 14' 6" high body in October 1944, complete with dull red paint finish and wooden seats. The primitive design of the body, intended to be built with the minimum of skilled labour is obvious. The white bands around the trees (right-hand foreground) and the white markers on the rear of the other two buses were intended to assist drivers during the blackout which was rigorously enforced to prevent stray lights assisting enemy bombers.

27

When the Ministry of Supply agreed to the manufacture of wartime 'austerity' buses they laid down a strict specification accompanied by drawings. For example, wood framing was to be used to save metal, with this body framing forming the window pillars. Only one opening window was permitted on each side of each deck, but ventilators were to be fitted to the front upstairs windows. One destination box was permitted but the upstairs rear 'window' had to be a sheet of metal, while no lining panels whatsoever were permitted inside except that the front of each deck could be trimmed with (if available) linoleum or compressed cardboard. Initially some seating comfort was allowed but slatted wooden seats soon became the norm, as did the harsh rectangular domes front and back, panel beaters work being kept to the absolute minimum. The first prototype was completed by Park Royal in September 1941 and in modified form, production continued until 1946.

The second pattern of Guy chassis to be built was, logically enough, the Arab II, being modified from the original to accept any engines available at any time.   Both of these illustrations show Guy Arab II, with Gardner 5LW engines, albeit the Birmingham vehicle has a Strachans body, and the Midland Red machines Park Royal bodywork, both being new in 1945.   The difference is that BCT No. 1401 was never rebuilt and withdrawn after only five years service, whereas 2584 and her sisters were rebuilt by Brush in 1950/51 with, as shown, rubber mounted windows, a considerable increase in ventilation and that curious built up front end.   However, the play of light on the side of 2584 suggests that all is not well in the framing.   The vibration of the Gardner five-cylinder engine was rather bad and the necessity for drivers to thrash these machines to keep time led to their withdrawal in 1955.

In Birmingham, a sense of stability kept the Corporation fleet almost entirely from purchasing unorthodox vehicles. They may have essayed a trial with Morris-Commercial, but not for BCT such oddities as the AEC Q, with its side mounted engine, or the ill-fated Wulfrunian which built-in too many clever ideas. Instead with both trams and buses they progressed gently leaving it to other concerns to winkle out the bugs in new designs. And their orders were worthwhile. CVP 157 was one of a batch of 100 Daimler COG5 chassis ordered in 1936 and delivered from the body builder, Metro-Cammell of Saltley in 1937. In all 206 buses were supplied that year; all except 5 Leyland and 5 AEC machines were COG5/MCW 54 seaters. 1057, like many of her sisters was withdrawn in 1952.

In many ways Cumberland Motor Services Ltd., were mavericks within the orderly PSV industry. It was a Tilling Group company but enough shares were held by private interests to ensure that the dead (or dead-ish) hand of conformity did not apply to their vehicle purchases. They should have bought Bristol/ECW products but although outvoted from September 1948 (after nationalisation), forward ordering allowed ten similar buses, one of the classic designs of all times, to enter service in 1952. A Leyland 53 seat lowbridge body graces a Leyland PD2/12 chassis. The destination blind has an unusual use, to indicate the type of service (workmen) rather than a geographical location.

The typically British double deck bus eventually evolved into a quite unique machine. Viewing many of the old Corporation run fleets some commentators have claimed the design had fossilized by the 1950s and one has to admit that if a company announced it was going to build a bus with the engine on the roof neither the engineer or his transport committee were going to get excited and rush off to buy ten. Instead they would send for their usual chassis and body builders, look at the modifications they had made to last year's model, agree a price (which had to be competitive) and that was that. The advantage of this policy was that only a handful of spare part bins were required and when the driver rang up to say his grockle-chaser had fallen off the thrumble pin the fitter knew he required a widget (plus a hammer) and that widget would fit most, if not all, of the fleet. As an example of conservatism Daimler delivered the CVG-type chassis until 1968 - but the "V" stood for victory, having been introduced in 1946.

Three from Northampton, all in pleasant red and cream and seen the same day.

JVV 211, a Daimler CVG6 with Roe 59 seat body delivered 1959.

ANH 175, a Daimler CVG6 with Roe 56 seat body delivered 1949.

ANH 165 coming up behind is a Daimler CVG6 with Northern Coach Builders 56 seat body delivered 1947.

However, to prove there can be change - JVV has a glass fibre radiator surround!

R.H.G. Simpson

Primarily due to the presence of existing rail bridges or canal aqueducts there has always been a requirement for low height buses. The use of single deck vehicles was totally uneconomic in tramway days leading to the premature cessation of services by some companies.

In bus days where heavy traffic was offered concentrated in short peaks single deck vehicles seating no more than 40 required the same crew as a 56 seat double decker, so much design work went into producing suitable bodies; ending up with the four in a row upstairs seat having a sunken side gangway.

Just how severe a low bridge problem could be is shown here. The notice reads:

DANGER
Double deck omnibuses
STOP
Conductor to see road clear

and the photograph at Wey Hill is dated March 1965. The vehicle is No.890 (EOT 27) in the Aldershot & District fleet, a Guy Arab II originally equipped with a utility body in 1945, but refitted by East Lancashire with a low height 56 seat body in 1954.

M. Norton

Charles Terres Weymann, a Franco-American, started research into a 'non-squeak' car body before World War I, patented the design in 1920 and opened his UK Factory in 1926, absorbing the Cunard Motor & Carriage Company in that year. Their Addlestone factory, where they were to stay until December 1965 opened in 1927. The principle behind the Weymann body was that there was no wood to wood contact at the joints. In 1932 they united in a trading deal with Metropolitan-Cammell Carriage, Wagon & Finance Co.Ltd., to form what we now know as MCW. Charles Weymann himself resigned in 1932, and in 1933, the Weymann factory completed its first all metal body, on an AEC Regent chassis for the City of Oxford Motor Service Ltd. In 1952, on an AEC Regent III chassis they completed fleet number 175, TWL 175, for the City of Oxford M.S. fleet. 175, of lowbridge construction, with a sunken gangway at the side, is seen in August 1962.

Resplendent in a cream livery with a light blue upper deck MKH77 of the East Yorkshire Motor Services fleet was almost new when photographed in 1952. The orthodox Leyland PD2/12 chassis is hidden by a unique style of bodywork manufactured by Charles H. Roe of Leeds. This was unique insofar as it combined a full front, coach seats and rear platform doors with the Beverley Bar taper. To add to the ensemble, the use of canted upper deck sliding windows was required due to the 8' 0" width of the body; earlier 7' 6" bodywork was able to be parallel to the cantrail level.

After two years in this special livery MKH77 was repainted in the normal dark blue and cream 'service' colours. She is seen on the parking ground opposite Wellington Street Bus Station, Leeds, where 'spare' vehicles awaited their return working. The notice on the wall of the now demolished Central Station gives details of August Bank Holiday train trips to Cleethorpes from Leeds. The Beverley 'Bar' which enforced the tapered roof design of all 170 East Yorkshire double deck vehicles in the 1950s was a Gothic arch that barred entry to the town. From 1971 onwards when a new by-pass gave alternative access standard vehicles could be purchased.

The classical timeless elegance of an AEC Regent III coupled to a Park Royal 56-seater body.   Built in 1952 she was No. 490 (PVT 936) in the Potteries Motor Traction Company's fleet, and not sold out of service until 1965.   490 was in fact an unlicensed demonstrator prior to purchase by PMT in June 1952, and was taken out of service to be displayed at the Commerical Motor Show in September that year on stand 74 when the chassis alone cost £2,570 albeit complete with tyres.

In 1956 Bedlington & District Luxury Coaches of Ashington, Northumberland, operated a fleet of ten double deck buses plus seven coaches, having eight AEC, four Leyland, two Daimler, two Foden and one Bedford chassis. Livery was maroon and light coach cream. By 1986 the fleet was twenty-one double and two single deck buses all painted mid coach green and light coach cream. Chassis were AEC and Leyland. Two photographs show part of the fleet in the 1960s.

In the top illustration 960 PRR is an unusual lowheight Northern Counties body on an AEC Regent V chassis ex-Barton Transport of Chilwell. LYR 851 is, like the vehicles in the lower photograph, an ex-London Transport 'RT' class vehicle in this case RT 3432. The lower photo shows (left to right) RTs 768, 2500, 4758 and 4696. All except 768 were ex-London Country and originally painted green and cream.

The rather apposite Bedlington dog is a rough working animal rather than a 'powder puff' show dog and of the breed which once played an important part in the lives of the older generation of miners; miners carried to work and back by Bedlington & District Luxury Coaches.

Judy-Joan Wright Collection

Browns Blue Coaches Ltd of Markfield, Leicestershire, started operations in 1923, and grew until between 1945 and 1963 (when they sold out to Midland Red) they were the largest independent operator in Leicestershire. In their time they owned at least 130 vehicles, most purchased secondhand, and still had 39 at the time of the takeover.

The purchase of previously-owned vehicles carried no shame with it in the PSV world, particularly when they came from reputable operators like London Transport. HLW 144 was once RT 157, an AEC Regent III with a Park Royal 56 seater body, new in 1948, and sold by London Transport not because of wear and tear but simply as they had an excess of vehicles following a loss of patronage.

GUT 398, on the other hand, had a Leyland Royal Tiger chassis, and was new to Browns Blues in 1951. The bodywork, seating 41, was by Duple in their quite luxurious 'Roadmaster' model.

3908.

D14 (BRR 914) of the East Midland Motor Services fleet had quite a tale to tell. This low-height double decker entered service in 1936 with a Leyland 53 seat body on her Leyland 'Titan' TD4 chassis. Powered by a 8.6 litre diesel engine, the TD4 was, probably, the most useful chassis then available, giving 21' 5'' (6.53m) of load space, and having, at least, a good strong clutch. 100 of this model, with certain differences to suit London conditions, were sold to London Transport in 1937, with Leyland metal framed bodies. D14 after surviving the war, was damaged by fire in March 1946 and as they offered early delivery was sent to Charles Roberts of Wakefield for a new body, re-entering service in December. Incredibly D14 was then to remain available for work until 1960, 24 years after she left the Leyland factory.

40

Northern Coachbuilders commenced operations in 1932, during the worst slump known in Britain and at a rather unusual location; Newcastle-upon-Tyne. Until the war they did little more than survive although the workmanship of their composite (wood framed) motor bodies was high. During the war they were able to take advantage of being one of the few coach and bus body builders authorized by the Ministry of Supply to continue such work. Thus in the immediate post war period after completing an order for twenty trolleybus bodies for London Transport they were able to offer good delivery dates on new bodywork of the type shown here, a 1947 53 seat lowbridge design. The exterior with its mean sliding windows is rather uninspired but internally quality was high, with laquered wood inserts around the windows and polished metal framed seats. However, as a family concern, Northern Coachbuilders ran into financial problems not of their making and had to close their doors in 1950, after a less than twenty year life. The chassis is a Leyland PD1, the first postwar design from this manufacturer which was of 16' 3" (4.95m) wheelbase, used the 7.4 litre oil engine and had a constant mesh gearbox. Nearly 1500 were produced (in three home market variants) although fom late 1947 the PD2 using the 0.600 diesel and a synchromesh box became available.

Glasgow, at least in 1963, covered an area of 61 square miles and had a resident population of just over one million. To transport this number the City had had 1150 tramcars operating over a maximum route mileage of 134. The first electric car ran in October 1898, the last September 1962. The first motor bus service operated from Monteith Row to Maryhill on 8 December 1924. But for years buses were regarded as nothing more than feeders to tramcars, and the first major tramway closure was not until 1948. But by 1963 trams were gone, replaced by 1334 motorbuses and 178 trolleybuses. DR11 on route 12 from St. Enoch Square via Gorbals Street to Toryglen has a wartime Daimler CWA (Commercial, Wartime, AEC [engine]) chassis, which was originally fitted with a utility body by Pickering of Wishaw. Built 1944, by 1954 this was 'ripe' and replaced by the East Lancs 58 seat body seen here. The clear number blinds were a bonus! Although withdrawn in 1959 she continued in use as a driver trainer for another six years.

L129 a Leyland PD2/24 was delivered as a bare chassis to Coplawhill Car Works (from whence came that most beautiful of all tramcars, the Cunarder) in 1958. There the workmen, anxious to show that they could build a decent bus body when given the chance, erected the elegant 61 seat machine shown here. Built to Alexander design, rather oddly some years later plates appeared purporting to show SGD31 (one of 100 from the Car Works) had been built by Alexander. The majority of the buses to the rear of L129 are Albions, but the two on the left hand side are, themselves, differing types of Albion! FYS 517, B135, extreme left, has an Albion Venturer CX37SW chassis of 1953, with a Weymann body. DGB 454, BR21 ex 806, has a wartime (1940) Albion Venturer CX19 chassis, originally fitted with a Pickering body, but re-bodied in 1952 by East Lancs, giving at least a semblance of newness.

The AEC Regent V chassis was one of the last to be produced in considerable numbers before the front loading/rear engined type of vehicle was to virtually sweep away dual crewed buses. East Kent bought 161 'Regents' between 1959 and 1967, all with variations on this rather severe, almost rectangular Park Royal 72 seat body. The upper deck windows are particularly shallow, especially as they worked in the tourist Herne Bay/Whitstable/Canterbury areas. The folding doors were often pinned open in summer, and driver/conductor co-operation and co-ordination seemed to make the latter's work easier than on a back-loader. 840 seen here as delivered in 1961, was withdrawn from East Kent service in 1976.

The M & D and East Kent Bus Club

LANDMARK - ATLANTEAN & FLEETLINE

The Leyland Atlantean changed the face of British double deck buses almost literally 'at a stroke'. Simply, the engine moved from sitting by the driver's left elbow, turned 90° and ended up at the back of the vehicle. From having two men serving the public, only one was to remain as now the fare paying passengers (or most of them) had to file past his outstretched hand. There were problems, due partially to hitherto unknown stresses put on bodywork, and the drivers no longer having the engine near them promptly forgot their existence and no tishy 2" dial is ever going to have the same impact as a waft of steam entering the cab! And, indeed, with fare collection, deteriorating driver/customer relationships (for suddenly the drivers were as vulnerable as the conductor had always been) and apalling traffic congestion if that 2" dial had been 12" and wore a tu-tu it is unlikely to have been noticed. Heating on early Atlanteans was almost non-existent for those enormously long pipework runs precluded what should only be hottish water reaching the cab, and indeed often overcooled the engine. Draughts were no less though! Mechanically, with no space between engine, gearbox, transfer box and wheels, the garage night-fitters suddenly faced their worst dreams. A certain degree of 'whip' and indeed misalignment between drive components was quite normal for traditional vehicles, with a handful of bearers and two or more universal joints absorbing and taming this. Now instead of 15'-16' to play in, the whole forces were concentrated in 4', and the drive not only went the 'wrong' way, but, to keep floor levels down and to make the best of what space there was, the shaft was angled from engine to axle - shown by the dotted lines in the drawing. Prior to the introduction of the Atlantean, six makers produced 11 distinctly different models of 'proper' buses, while by 1968, the Leyland Atlantean of 1958, Daimler Fleetline (1960) and Bristol VRT (1967) fought for orders. A year later, it has to be said, having gained control of Bristol, the British Leyland Group had a monopoly; spare part deliveries were so bad that VOR (Vehicle Off Road) statistics could show a vehicle on shed for up to six months and operators were commonly allowing a float of 20-25% spare buses, against 8% for traditional back-loaders. The outline drawing dates back to 1966.

The first production Leyland Atlantean demonstrator appeared in 1959, but only a year later Daimler put their Fleetline on show. It was to be six years after that before the Bristol VR was made available to would-be buyers. In theory therefore the Atlantean should have mopped up most orders and the Fleetline the rest. But the Leyland product had the disadvantage of not being a true low-height machine whereas the Fleetline emphatically was, being built complete with full length 'proper' centre gangway on both decks as low as 13' 5" (4.11m) overall. Additionally the Fleetline used the economical engineers favourite engine, the Gardner LX. The low height was attained by the use of a drop-centre pattern of rear axle, although the mechanical complications inherent in any rear engine rear drive machine made operation of early model buses interesting.

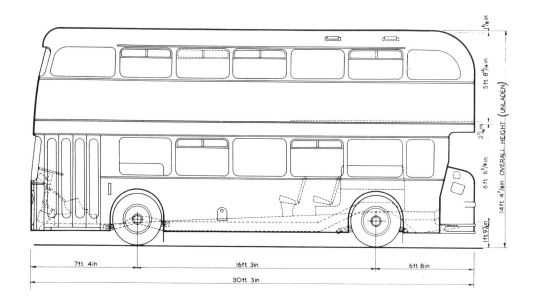

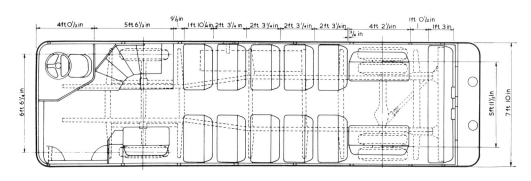

7ft 4in   16ft 3in   6ft 8in

30ft 3in

5ft 8¹¹⁄₁₆in   2⁷⁄₁₆in   6ft 6³⁄₈in   1ft 9³⁄₁₆in

1³⁄₈in

14ft 4⁷⁄₈in OVERALL HEIGHT (UNLADEN)

4ft 0½in   5ft 6½in   9½in   1ft 10¼in   2ft 3¼in   2ft 3¼in   2ft 3¼in   2ft 3¼in   4ft 2½in   1ft 0½in

¾in   1ft 3in

6ft 6¼in

5ft 11½in   7ft 10in

46

Perhaps justifiably this particular variant of the Atlantean has been described as the most attractive of all. Certainly the panoramic windows of the Alexander full height coach-seated body add a sleekness to what is really only a box on wheels, and the slight streamlining of the upper deck shows a stylist's attention. Just six of this chassis/bodywork permutation were delivered to Lothian Regional Transport, subsequently bearing the names of Scotsmen including 'Robert Burns' as shown here.

In its heyday the combined tram, trolley and omnibus fleets of Birmingham Corporation Transport were probably unequalled among provincial operators, due to a very large extent to the standards of maintenance and that the BCT engineers moved very slowly towards modernization. One, answering a query over the old-fashioned appearance of their new Guy Arabs, asked why change should be made when the old served their needs?

Eventually in 1969 Birmingham was forcibly absorbed into the West Midlands Passenger Transport Authority and, perforce, bought front-loader, rear engined vehicles but to encourage local industry the P.T.E. purchased the MCW Metrobus in its various forms. 2387 (LOA 387X) a 1982 DR 102/22 model seating 73 within its rather boxy shell, is seen turning into Liverpool Street garage, effectively bridging the gap between tradition as exemplified by the Coat-of-Arms and a modern bus.

Kevin Lane

Variations on a box.
YNA 363M, Midland Red (South) ex Greater Manchester PTE Daimler
CRG6LXB/Northern Counties.
Note the skylights brightening the upper deck.
SDA 715S (with doors closed) G & G Travel ex West Midlands PTE Leyland
FE30AGR/MCW
G & G are an Associated Company of Midland Red (South)
A 541HAC new to Midland Red (South) Leyland ONLXB/ECW
The Olympian was Leyland's swansong.
There *are* wheels, deep October shadows loose them.

When the new bus station at Tavistock was opened in 1957 what better vehicle as an advertisement for Western National than 1929, an almost brand new Eastern Coach Works 60 seat bodied Bristol LD6B, one of the famous Lodekkas of which, adding together all the production variants, 5213 were built between 1953 and 1966. In all 2179 "pure" LDs appeared and in their time they were quite revolutionary for the combination of a drop-centre rear axle and a very lowslung chassis eliminated the step into the saloon and banished the problem of having reasonable - or even legal - headroom on both decks without recourse to side gangways. In this case 1929 was Bristol powered, although the Gardner engines were available and of particular note is the white steering wheel used to remind drivers the bus was to the then new 8' 0" width. 1929 was withdrawn in May 1976 but let us remember her at Tavistock with the white ribbon (visible on the left) still fluttering in the breeze.

Within the North West, as elsewhere, the advent of the National Bus Company led to some previous rivals, however unwillingly, becoming bed-fellows. One Managing Director is supposed to have said that for another (named) company to be united with his was like putting fleas on a pedigree dog. Crosville, North Western, Ribble & Cumberland Motor Services became as one, and although before 1969, the 'unifying' date, CMS had had to abandon their preferred Leylands for Bristols nonetheless they were still a separate entity both physically and within the minds of the staff. The Bristol Lodekka was very much a 'standard' Tilling Group vehicle whether front or rear loading but the CMS machines always seemed to be that little better maintained, even the wheelnuts retaining their bright finish long after many companies would have painted them along with the wheels.

The first Bristol VR models had their engines placed longitudinally at the rear behind the axle thus in theory giving the advantage of excellent access and a more orthodox drive, albeit back-to-front compared with the traditional engine at the front. The first prototype utilized a Gardner LX and appeared at the 1966 Commercial Motor Show. By 1968 when production got under way, three types of Gardner engine were offered, two Leyland and, rather oddly, the AEC AV691. Two engine locations were possible, lengthwise or transversely as in the Atlantean. Both high- and low-bridge chassis were available and two wheel-base lengths. The primary advantage of the VR from an engineers viewpoint, apart from the general exellence of Bristol workmanship, was that the radiator was located at the front of the chassis, far from the heat and vibration of the engine. With further variations the VR was to stay in production until August 1981 as the last 'true' Bristol designed double deck chassis, as from September 1969 50% of the Company's shares were held by British Leyland and from early 1983 Bristol became a wholly owned subsidiary. BL could hardly tolerate another vehicle design being considered better than their own so the Bristol works closed after 75 years of production from the first petrol engined bus delivered 12 May 1908 to the last diesel in November 1983. An Eastern Coach Works body is fitted to this 'typical' bus and one which is regarded as of classical design being both simple and balanced. The white window rubbers added some elegance and the use of fibreglass panels kept maintenance costs to a reasonable level. Seating (according to the model chosen) could be as high as 83, but, for example, a batch built as double deck motorway coaches for Ribble only held 60, 18 in the lower saloon, 42 above. In 1986, following the sale of Leyland Bus to its management, the ECW works at Lowestoft, bus and coach builders since 1920, not being included, was closed. This particular machine, No.27, XDL 377L, was a Bristol VRTSL (Transverse, Short Length) [mk] 2 - 6LX (Gardner engine) with ECW full height body seating 74.

These Bristol VR/ECW bodied machines are in the fleet of Eagles & Crawford, Mold, Clwyd and are included to show some of the variations that can occur even in a standardized machine. For example, the second vehicle (NUD 109L) has coach seating and different light fittings - particularly the 'flashers', to her sister NCD 561M, the last but one vehicle. RLG 292P, in the middle, is quite lopsided having had one upper deck opening light replaced by plain glass. GNJ 573N, far right has a two part windscreen, NCD one big sheet of glass. Add five different blind arrangements and there is a veritable pot pourri of mechanical magnificence!

After a series of upmarket double deck buses Ribble's coaching subsidiary W C Standerwick commissioned a batch of Weymann bodied Leyland Atlantean PDR 1/1 chassis. Only seating 59 these vehicles were fitted with a toilet and a servery which initially offered airline-style hot meals although later only hot drinks and snacks were available. Numbered 16 - 48 in the fleet they led the way to the later Bristols used on the same Lancashire-London routes. Seats in these "Gay Hostess" coaches were individually adjustable and the main lights could be dimmed at night while a P.A. system was the height of modernity when they were delivered during 1959-1961, air suspension on the front making for an easy ride.

1. Daimler
2. A.E.C.
3. B.M.M.O.
4. Renault
5. Austin
6. Guy
7. A.E.C.

BUILDING BUSES - '30s STYLE

Strachan and Brown, Coach Builders, Wales Farm Road, Acton W3 pretty well says it all. About 20 bodies varying from little market buses to double deckers are visible. The chassis in the foreground is a Dennis, probably an E type built to 'Scotland Yard' requirements, far from new, another is at the rear of the workshops. To show how labour intensive such a works could be at least 83 men (including the gaffers in the foreground) are visible.

The photograph of Chiswick Works shows vehicles of the ST (Short T) being completed in 1930. The second from right is probably ST 571, in all 1139 'ST' type chassis were built, their bodies seating 49.

R.W. Kidner

Travel with friends

Two photographs from the camera of Roger Kidner. LT 561 was seen at the AEC test ground in the works at Southall, January 1932. It was the LT (Long T) class three axle (six-wheel) omnibus that was to be immortalized by Flanders & Swann. The chassis, as the AEC Renown, was first introduced in 1929, and had a 16' 6" (5.05m) wheelbase. The first prototype completed vehicle commenced work on the 6 August. From LT 151 onwards the format was fixed at 56 seat composite body with an enclosed staircase (to the relief of small boys petrified by the sight of the road whizzing away beneath them), powered by a 6 cylinder overhead camshaft petrol engine developing 91 b.h.p. from its 6.1 litres. The lion's share of bodywork came from Chiswick Works and although there were many variations in detail, all bar a handful of early ones were interchangeable from chassis to chassis. The last double-deck 'LT' to remain in revenue earning service left from Upton Park Garage on 12 January 1950.

Two photographs of double deck construction believed to have been either at Strachans of Acton or Brush of Loughborough, the balance of probabilities being in favour of the former.

Construction details are quite fascinating, in the left hand corner of the upper photograph three stages in roof building from skeleton, to planked state through to the aluminium skin are obvious while behind traditional wood framing of a body top deck takes shape. The single deckers on the right appear to date back to the 1930s but they may be in for repair or re-bodying.

The lower photograph shows how the cab framework was built up later, the Leyland PD2 on the left looking very odd without it. The protruding ventilators, often so fitted on a lowheight body were shockingly vulnerable to any boskage that overhung the road and, moreover, leaked very badly.

This photograph is rather unusual insofar as it shows the completed upper deck of a 'camel back' roofed bus built by Strachans in 1929 on a Thornycroft HC-type 3 axle chassis, presumably with an eye to export orders as the full height sliding windows would have little use on a November's day in Aldershot.

The principle behind the camel back design, which for about five years was adopted by most manufacturers is that the shallow roof allowed passage under low bridges, or at least reduced the propensity of drivers to forget where the corners were, while still allowing a reasonable headroom along the aisle. It was an inherently weak structure and very prone to leakage.

Unfortunately, we do not know which chassis is being bodied here, although we do know it is a corner of the workshops in Wales Farm Road, Acton, London W3, that was utilized by Strachans (Action)Ltd (ex Strachan & Brown) and that the date is around 1930/1.

As can be seen the basic structure is in wood and that unlike some other manufacturers Strachans did not try to bend the wood frames in a steam chest but cut them irregardless of the grain. The floor is in deal and the horizontal members crossing the photograph are merely temporary braces although the longitudinal members are all in situ. Prominent is the well forming the gangway beside the four-in-a-row seats.

Metal Sections of Oldbury were world-famous for their provision of vehicles in "knock-down" condition to the Colonies and other foreign parts. The whole design of their export bus shells was so cleverly thought out that packaging costs were kept to a minimum and assembly by semi-skilled labour relatively easy. On one occasion the drawings were impounded by local officials looking for a helping of baksheesh (bribes) but nothing daunted the garage mechanics not only assembled the bus shells on the quayside but drove them away!

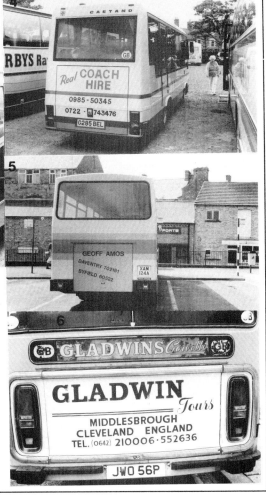

ASPECTS OF OMNIBUSES 2
BLUNT ENDS

1. U.C.O.C.
2. Duple
3. Harrington
4. Caetano
5. Reeve Burgess
6. Plaxton

VILLAGE BUS OR LUXURY COACH

The 4-ton Bristol bus chassis entered production at the Motor Constructional Works, Brislington during 1920, as a brand new design owing little or nothing to pre-war models. Fitted with a Bristol BW type 4 cylinder petrol engine of 32.4 h.p. standard Bristol-built bodywork normally seated 30 passengers. The Yorkshire (West Riding) Tramways Company, based at Wakefield, had found their passenger traffic badly battered by the prolonged miners' strikes of 1921, while their trackwork was equally battered by subsidence and passing heavy waggons who found their lines a much more level surface to run on than the surrounding quagmires that passed as roads. Small wonder, then, that in January 1922 the Tramway Company decided to set up a bus operating arm, particularly as these vehicles could go to villages where no tram went. What was surprising was their choice of Bristol chassis, but moving quickly deliveries began in February 1922, and within three years their trading division, The West Riding Automobile Company, had around 200 vehicles in their fleet, the last Yorkshire (West Riding) trams running back on-shed 25 July 1932.

On the back of the photograph is an inscription written in an educated hand "Castleford. Saturday 15th July 1922 Four of these buses, garage built to hold 8".

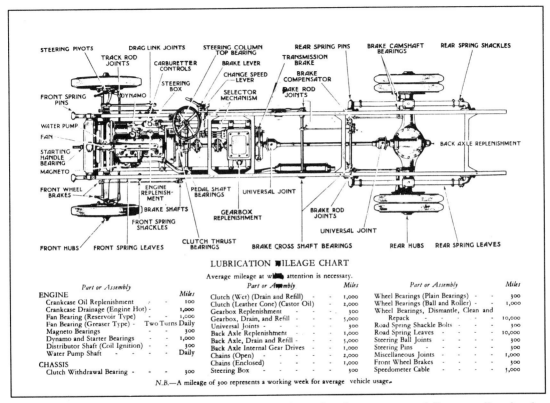

STEERING PIVOTS — DRAG LINK JOINTS — STEERING COLUMN TOP BEARING — REAR SPRING PINS — BRAKE CAMSHAFT BEARINGS — REAR SPRING SHACKLES — TRACK ROD JOINTS — CARBURETTER CONTROLS — BRAKE LEVER — TRANSMISSION BRAKE — CHANGE SPEED LEVER — BRAKE COMPENSATOR — STEERING BOX — SELECTOR MECHANISM — BRAKE ROD JOINTS — FRONT SPRING PINS — DYNAMO — WATER PUMP — FAN — STARTING HANDLE BEARING — MAGNETO — BACK AXLE REPLENISHMENT — FRONT WHEEL BRAKES — ENGINE REPLENISHMENT — PEDAL SHAFT BEARINGS — UNIVERSAL JOINT — BRAKE SHAFTS — GEARBOX REPLENISHMENT — BRAKE ROD JOINTS — FRONT SPRING SHACKLES — UNIVERSAL JOINT — FRONT HUBS — FRONT SPRING LEAVES — CLUTCH THRUST BEARINGS — BRAKE CROSS SHAFT BEARINGS — REAR HUBS — REAR SPRING LEAVES

LUBRICATION MILEAGE CHART

Average mileage at which attention is necessary.

Part or Assembly	Miles	Part or Assembly	Miles	Part or Assembly	Miles
ENGINE		Clutch (Wet) (Drain and Refill)	1,000	Wheel Bearings (Plain Bearings)	300
Crankcase Oil Replenishment	100	Clutch (Leather Cone) (Castor Oil)	2,000	Wheel Bearings (Ball and Roller)	1,000
Crankcase Drainage (Engine Hot)	1,000	Gearbox Replenishment	300	Wheel Bearings, Dismantle, Clean and	
Fan Bearing (Reservoir Type)	1,000	Gearbox, Drain, and Refill	5,000	Repack	10,000
Fan Bearing (Greaser Type)	Two Turns Daily	Universal Joints	300	Road Spring Shackle Bolts	300
Magneto Bearings	300	Back Axle Replenishment	1,000	Road Spring Leaves	10,000
Dynamo and Starter Bearings	1,000	Back Axle, Drain and Refill	5,000	Steering Ball Joints	300
Distributor Shaft (Coil Ignition)	300	Back Axle Internal Gear Drives	1,000	Steering Pins	300
Water Pump Shaft	Daily	Chains (Open)	2,000	Miscellaneous Joints	1,000
CHASSIS		Chains (Enclosed)	1,000	Front Wheel Brakes	300
Clutch Withdrawal Bearing	300	Steering Box	300	Speedometer Cable	5,000

N.B.—A mileage of 300 represents a working week for average vehicle usage.

It is very difficult for the average motorist, whether driving privately or commercially, to realize the sheer hard work involved in keeping early vehicles on the road. This chassis outline probably dates back to the early 1920s and was produced by the predecessor company to the Mobiloil group of today. As a working day of 12-14 hours was commonplace for the owner/driver maintenance other than replenishment of oil and water had to be carried out on Sunday. Even in the 1950s one company put aside Saturday for overhauls since the coaches were used for Sunday excursions, but should there be a demand for a vehicle to convey a cricket or rugby team or group of supporters on the Saturday the driver was expected to carry out greasing, oil changes and heavy cleaning at night after his day's run.

The first Tillings-Stevens petrol-electric buses type TTA2 were delivered to the Birmingham & Midland Motor Omnibus Company Ltd ('Midland Red') in 1913, but a year before this a Tillings-bodied demonstrator running on trade plates (DG 452) was shown around the Harborne area. The primary advantage of a petrol electric design was that the ex-tram or horse-bus driver had no necessity to learn to handle a gear-box. The plain truth is that very many of these men had no affinity with mechanical machinery and apart from the horrendous noises that could and can be made in an early gear-box, wear and tear meant breakdowns and delays, let alone vexed passengers who were often both shaken and stirred enough to write to **The Times**.

There were two prices to pay for simplicity in control. By no stretch of the imagination could any Tillings-Stevens be called fast or lively and fuel consumption was fairly dreadful. Still, some of them gave ten years strenuous service while running on average 600 miles per week at the regulation 12 m.p.h.

East Pennine Transport Group

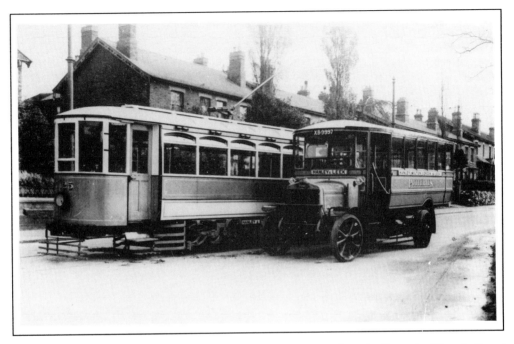

Proudly emblazened on the side of XB 9997 was the name "Potteries" short for Potteries Electric Traction Company and it is this, as much as the tram, that showed where their heart really lay. XB 9997 was numbered 36 in the P.E.T. fleet and came from Samuelson New Transport, a London-based coach operator, in 1922. She originally carried a Strachan & Brown charabanc body on a Daimler Y-type chassis, itself ex W.D., but was re-bodied some time before sale. 36 was withdrawn in 1929, by which time she was long outclassed by modern vehicles.

Tram 125 was built in 1920 at the Tividale Works of the Birmingham & Midland Tramways Joint Committee. Acquired new as a sample car she was one of a batch of 11, six going to the Dudley and Stourport line and four to the Wolverhampton District Electric Tramways Company.

When photographed here in 1922 she seated 32 passengers in rather more comfort than the 29 of the bus. The last P.E.T. tramcar ran on 11 July 1928.

East Pennine Transport Group

FM 2365, Crosville Motor Services No. 82 had a Leyland chassis classified as 36G7, although pedantically it should have been 36SG7, the driver sitting alongside the engine (S = side-type) rather than behind it. The bodywork, seating 40, including 2 alongside the driver, was also by Leyland, and had a full height partition behind the driver and two saloons divided by doors.

82 entered service in 1923, the date of this photograph, received pneumatic tyres in the mid-1920s thus increasing her legal speed from 12 to 20 mph but was withdrawn in 1930.

She represents a particular era in Public Service Vehicle construction, with a high chassis, 4-speed sliding mesh gearbox and worm driven straight rear axle.   The wheelbase was 16' 6" (5.03m) and the overall length 27' 5" (8.36m).   The half outside/half inside position of the 4 cylinder 36-40 h.p. engine is reminiscent of the Bedford CF series coaches.

But, more important than the technical specification are the clearly evident influences on the bodywork styling.   The lifeguards and pivoted opening lights come from tramcars, visible on the original are railway-type torpedo ventilators, and the 'porch' doorways could belong to a Pullman car.

The steps are fearfully vulnerable but essential.   Electric lighting was very unreliable, so additional acetylene lamps were fitted.   These worked by the immersion of calcium carbide in water which produced acetylene gas and, once lit, this gave (gives indeed!) a very hard white light of around 100 candle power.

In 1993 few operators consider anything with less than 40 seats to be a real, economic 'big bus' and where mini- or midi-buses are used tend to keep them for shorthaul work with, all too often converted van shell bodywork, and drivers paid a lower hourly rate than their real bus colleagues. Once the idea of a small bus was to enable it to run in a driver only configuration and that meant less than 20 seats, but it did not have the corollary of rattly, shoddy or spartan bodywork, for many of these country buses would have a run of 30 miles or more.

This beautiful little Ford received its John Taylor (Barnsley Motor Bodies) body in 1926 and in all ways it was a comfortable bus of the latest design - just miniaturized!

During her lifetime Mona M. Morgan has seen the coming of the first charabancs to Radnorshire and she tells us how "by slow degrees motor transport came to our district in the late 1920s, to change and ultimately transform our lives . . . It was the market-bus that brought most benefit and pleasure, especially to small-holders and cottagers who had previously been obliged to walk to town on market days . . . The bus ride itself was no match for an open-air trap ride on a fine day. It was the company that everyone so enjoyed. Market journeys were jolly, social occasions, rather like day-trips, with friendly, animated country folk laughing and joking and calling to each other across the bus. Everyone was welcomed aboard with nods and smiles of greeting and a quip or two from the wits. The drivers were cheerful, willing chaps, ready to carry messages or undertake shopping orders for all and sundry. Farmers' wives came laden with baskets of poultry, butter and eggs . . . On the return journey, baskets laden with provisions were stacked aboard, everyone lending a hand. News gathered during the day was shared and lively animated talk echoed around. The eyes of the market-piert were a touch brighter than normal, their loosened tongues additionally entertaining. All passengers alighted to goodbyes, good wishes and jocular advice on how to conduct themselves in the coming days. In later years city folk on holiday in the district were fascinated by the market journeys. They were mystified when, for no apparent reason, the driver pulled up at a field gate, until they heard him remark, after several minutes, 'No sign o' Mrs Jones yet, but she'll be 'ere in a minute, sure to'. As she was spotted running and panting with her heavy baskets some might jocularly shout, 'Come on, Mrs. Jones, pierten-up or it'll be time to come back afore we gets there'. Climbing aboard she might say 'Ow long you bin waitin', Jack? Our clock was stood and I didna know no aim what the time was'. Such a remark would invite a bit of leg-pulling from the men on board and some spirited rejoinders from Mrs. Jones.

There would probably be further waits at gates or road-junctions, to make sure no one was left behind. Perhaps some one would be waiting to hand the driver a shopping-list, with the request 'Please to bring these few things for me, Jack'', sure of a willing response. To city folk it seemed so friendly and matey and, though unfamiliar with the local parlance, they loved the fun and repartee, and many were forced to revise their previous concept of the countryside as a dull and lonely place in which to live.''

The relevance to the building of Britain's buses is that without passengers vehicle improvements are stultified. Miles apart, none-the-less both the Daimler and the Tillings-Stevens took their turns carrying the local equivalent of Mrs. Morgan from the country to the town, and from the farmhouse to the market. Their travel encouraged others and led to today's smart, clean and bright Dennis or Leyland on the same services.

Early in 1992, an AEC Reliance with Duple bodywork, YPL 89T belonging to Phillips of Bobblestock, Hereford, was photographed waiting at Hereford for her morning working on route 440 to Abbeydore in the Golden Valley via Pontrilas. In many ways this vehicle is the lineal descendant of Mrs. Morgans market bus and is serving much the same area of country-side.

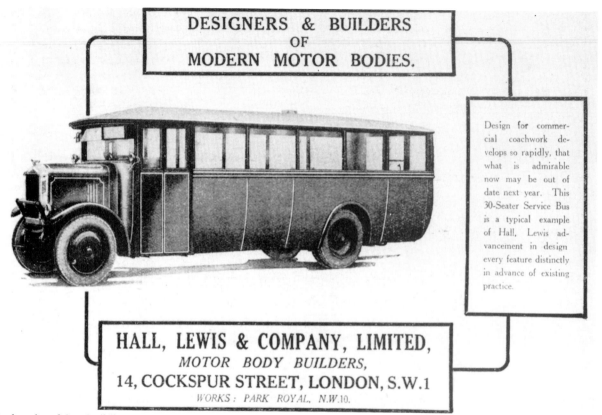

DESIGNERS & BUILDERS OF MODERN MOTOR BODIES.

Design for commercial coachwork develops so rapidly, that what is admirable now may be out of date next year. This 30-Seater Service Bus is a typical example of Hall, Lewis advancement in design every feature distinctly in advance of existing practice.

HALL, LEWIS & COMPANY, LIMITED,
MOTOR BODY BUILDERS,
14, COCKSPUR STREET, LONDON, S.W.1
WORKS : PARK ROYAL, N.W.10.

A decade of bus-building progress 1925-1935. Hall, Lewis were later to be re-formed as Park Royal Vehicles famed as builders of London's bus bodies. Charles H. Roe remained an independent, but major player in the game until 1948. In 1962 the ACV combine which by now included both Park Royal and Roe merged with the Leyland group. From the ashes of this came Optare whose address remains Crossgate Carriage Works, Leeds - a linear descendant of Hall Lewis & Roe alike - and who are right in the forefront of modern designs.

ONE OF A LARGE NUMBER TO THE DESIGN OF THE BRITISH ELECTRICAL
FEDERATION SUPPLIED TO THE HEBBLE MOTOR SERVICES.

TROLLEY
BUS
BODIES

CHAS. H. ROE L^{TD.}

CROSSGATES CARRIAGE WORKS

LEEDS

C.I. AND
PETROL
BUS
BODIES

Telephone : CROSSGATES 85182-3

Telegrams : " VEHICLES, LEEDS "

The *Gem* service was started in 1924 and ran from Derby (Bold Lane) to Quarndon Park Nook. Around 20 return services were run every day (except Sundays) and on 9 April 1931 this fast, light and economical Reo Speedwagon was acquired. This type of vehicle purchase was a feature of the late 1920s and early 1930s, with lightweight chassis by GMC, Reo, Lancia, Fiat, Berliet, and later, Bedford, almost invariably fitted with locally built rather skeletal bodies, serving country and outer urban localities. By their speed pioneering driver/operators were able to run circles around the lumbering "big operator"' Tillings-Stevens and Leylands chosen for their reliability, rather than manoeverability.

The drivers leather gaiters were probably necessary in the absence of a heater, but his smart uniform speaks of pride. The conductor has the ubiquitous Bell Punch ticket machine and vital cashbag.

The *Gem* service and their two Reos passed to *Kingfisher Services* in 1932, with *Kingfisher* in turn selling out to *Trent* on 24 March 1935.

John Heath

This rather severe 'frowning' style of Weymann body was not entirely appreciated by drivers as although advantageous on sunny days, the canopy reduced visibility in normal conditions.   Delivered in 1949 and seating 35 passengers, the bodywork however well built was almost immdediately outdated by the arrival of full fronted bus shells built on underfloor engined chassis.   The AEC Reliance (despite some problems) really killed off the Regal III chassis (type 6821A here) and H35 was withdrawn from the East Midland Motor Services fleet in 1960.   Most of the batch of nine saw a few years extra service with contractors, although H35s life after EMMS cannot be traced.   Seen here when almost new, the 'combination' tyre tread is slightly unusual.

The Commer 'Centurion' chassis was a very short lived model, first being made available in the Autumn of 1933, only to be withdrawn a year later. Although intended to carry 20 seat luxury coach bodywork most of the two dozen or so built became goods vehicles. The specification was quite advanced utilizing the reliable 22.6 h.p. 6 cylinder Commer petrol engine, a four speed gearbox, Bendix 'self-energising' brakes (i.e. servo operated and theoretically self adjusting) and a modern style single dry plate clutch. Bodywork in this show example is by Waveney Coachworks and contains every conceivable luxury for small party travel.

As Commercial Cars Ltd., Commer commenced vehicle manufacture in 1906 and for many years found their fortune lay in using an incredibly advanced pre-selector gearbox, first designed a year earlier. In 1926 they joined the Humber Group and with Karrier Motors provided the commercial arm of the Rootes Group until the takeover by Chrysler in 1964.

LANDMARK - TILLINGS-STEVENS B10

    The Tillings-Stevens B10 "Express" series were one of the most useful models of buses to operate in Britain. They were simple almost to the point of being utilitarian and a 1929 review makes this clear. They stated "Broadly considered, motor transport vehicle owners may be divided into two classes; those who do not think they get their money's worth in a chassis that does not bristle with 'Refinements' and those that know from unfortunate experience that every additional mechanical contrivance not only increases weight and cost, but probably requires periodical adjustment, lubrication and renewal of parts whilst interfering with accessibility. I can imagine the expressions of approval of the latter class when seeing the Express chassis for the first time. Though it would be incorrect to say that it possesses only bare necessities, since construction on such lines would leave many modern requirements unsatisfied, it is evident that its designers have followed a policy of elimination wherever efficiency, reliability, and convenience are not thereby sacrificed." The engine was a 'homely' little mechanism, having four cylinders "Two castings, separate detachable heads" with a bore of 108mm (4¼") and a stroke of 140 mm (5½") giving a capacity of 5130.11 cc. "For a vehicle of 32-passenger carrying capacity, the rated horse-power of the engine is decidedly below average" being 29 R.A.C. rating or 44.5 b.h.p. at 100 r.p.m. rising to 63.5 b.h.p. at a maximum 1500 r.p.m. "But those who doubted its ability to hold its own in the matter of speed on the level or up steep hills, or to withstand continuous hard slogging service on long-distance or local routes have told me that in these respects their judgment has proved to be at fault; the road performance capabilities of the vehicle have, in fact, compared favourably with others with engines of more pretentious dimensions". With the demand today for lower and lower floor heights to make vehicles more accessible it is odd to read that in 1929 "to be acceptable to the widest circle of users it is clearly undesirable for a passenger chassis to have too low a frame and for this reason a height of 2' 1¼" (64 cm) with 36" x 6" (91 x 15) tyres is well chosen".

    Brakes were primitive even by 1929 standards as "both hand and foot brakes retard the back wheels, the hand brake drums being 14½" (36.8cm) in diameter, and arranged inside the foot brake drums which are 21" (53.3cm) in diameter". The shoes were cam-operated, pivoted at the rear and 2½" (6.35cm) wide. However, "front wheel brakes and a servo unit can be fitted if desired". As these B10 vehicles were fairly widespread over the countryside one might have thought 4-wheel brakes useful in Derbyshire or Northumberland, let alone down Sun Rising or Gibbet Hills in the Home Counties! Bottom gear, however, had a ratio of 4.89 to 1 and coupled with a back axle ratio of 5.75 to 1 presumably enabled them to grind up and down 'Stately as a galleon'. The illustrations are designed to show all possible aspects of these machines.

In 1990 these two chassis and bodies were photographed at the Amberley Chalk Pits Museum, Sussex. On the left is UF 6805 ex Southdown fleet number 705, new as a B10C2 in 1930 with Short Brothers bodywork, sold 1939 to the War Department, and incredibly then survived as a chicken house until rescued for rebuilding.

MO 9324 on the right has the specially cast radiator top tank which proclaims her ownership. A B9A she was delivered in May 1927 with Brush bodywork and survived the war by being used on contract work carrying servicemen of all nationalities as well as civilian airfield and gunnery emplacement workers. The body is being steadily rebuilt from the wreck it was in 1983.

The chassis.

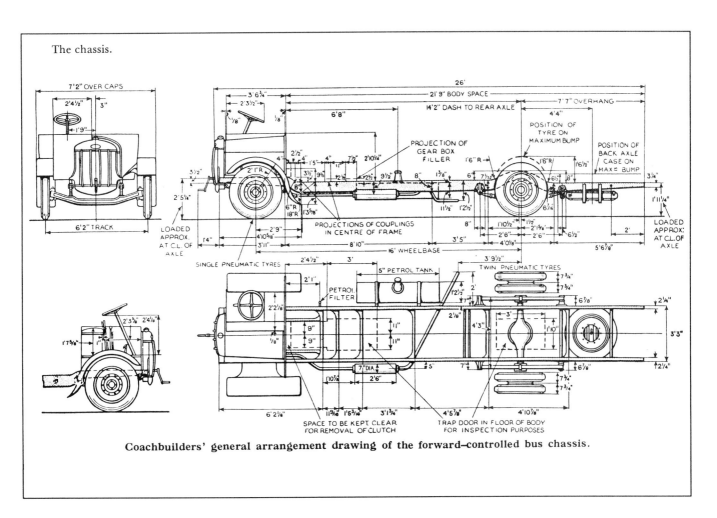

Coachbuilders' general arrangement drawing of the forward–controlled bus chassis.

77

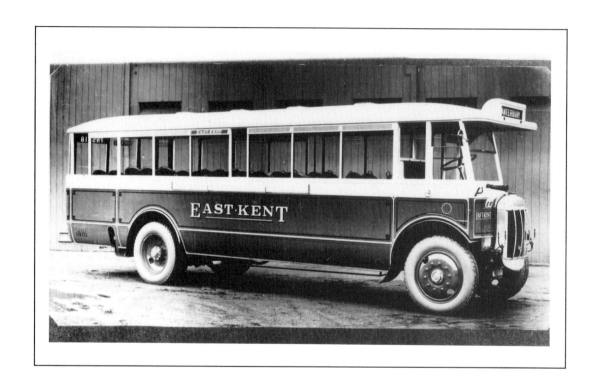

FN 9918 was a B10C2 with Brush bodywork seating 37 when delivered in February 1929. Withdrawn 1938 and may, like many Tillings-Stevens of the period, have ended her days with a showman at a fairground.

The M & D and East Kent Bus Club

FN 9942 was another B10C2 delivered in March 1929 but with Short Brothers of Rochester bodywork and to all intents and purposes virtually identical to FN 9918, although the location of bulkhead fittings varied and the radiator surround was polished. She was withdrawn in 1939 after quite an arduous ten years service and sold to a dealer in Leeds.

The M & D and East Kent Bus Club

In August 1930, Tillings-Stevens changed their name to T.S. Motors Ltd., ostensibly to sever the link with outmoded petrol-electrics. In practice they had broken away from the Tilling Group and wanted to show their independence. Unfortunately they also lost their main markets and were never to recover.

The C60A7 model celebrated their new freedom. Power came from a Ricardo-designed 6 cylinder engine of 6972cc developing 109.5 h.p. at 2500 r.p.m. This, alas, had a built-in flaw for only four main bearings were provided when seven were usual. The gearbox was remote from the engine (as in the B10) and is said to have yowled to such an extent that letters of complaint from householders were regularly received by operators. Four wheel brakes and a massive fully floating rear axle were excellent features but the clutch was weird as the friction plates were not fixed but floated freely. The idea was to simplify changing the plates but in practice they battered themselves to pieces and made gearchanging interesting.

39 were built, this is the demonstrator with bodywork by John C. Beadle of Dartford, providing a remarkable contrast with the B10 of two years previous. The curved glass was extremely rare in 1931.

All British bus and coach builders tended to be staid, solid companies, yet each at one time or another went 'off the rails', often to disastrous effect. Sunbeam had a Pathan model that lost them thousands of pounds, Gilford tried a front wheel drive diesel engined bus in the '30s which broke them, Albion tried an odd underfloor engined coach in the '50s, AEC the side engined Q type in 1932, Leyland rear engined buses in 1939, and so on.

This photograph of a beautiful Duple body is probably the rarest in this book for on the wheeltrims can be read "Tillings Stevens". Not TSM for they had gone back to the original name for their Successor model of 1937.

Two chassis were built. One was bodied. As far as can be checked neither moved under its own power. They tried to develop an 8-cylinder horizontally opposed direct injection diesel engine with wet type cylinder liners and a dry sump. The gearbox was fun, being a Maybach 7 speed with vacuum operated preselector gears. After that it just got plain complicated, typically suspension involved horizontal, note horizontal, coil springs. But what a magnificent perfectly balanced bodyshell.

Variations on Albion 'Valkyrie' chassis were to have a twenty year life as production models. The last variant was code-designated CX13, although this 'unlucky' number seems to have helped Albion survive the lean years of the late 1930s with steady sales for all three engine alternatives; Albion petrol 9.1 litre 6-cylinder, Albion oil 9.1 litre giving 15 m.p.g. and Gardner 8.4 litre 6LW. The advertisement dates back to 1935, the photograph shows a CX13 Valkyrie new to Red & White in 1947. Alas, the 35 seat Pickering body shown was far from robust and like its sisters had to be replaced within 5 or 6 years.

AHA 608 was one of the finest designs of 'proper' Midland "Red" coaches Motor Services. Built in 1935 with a Short Brothers of Rochester 30 seater coach body, the chassis bore the designation of SOS LRR (Low Rolls Royce). The 'Low' was an attempt to both reduce the centre of gravity and to make boarding easier for elderly or infirm passengers, while 'Rolls Royce' described the quality of ride expected. The body outline with the relatively high (and cramped!) cab was slightly quirky. The bald tyre would do little to encourage would-be passengers nowadays, but from 1940 608 and her sisters were converted to 34 seat buses and worked hard on the so-called 'dispersal' routes carrying 'Blitzed' citizens from their temporary country residences to their factories and also taking workmen to satellite works - Coventry to the Maudslay Works at Alcester was a typical run. As a bus 608 survived until 1951.

The use of the magic letters 'SOS' on every exposed surface is not, as is commonly thought, the reaction of a London driver seeing one of these vehicles but, probably, stood for "Shires Own Specification" or "Shires Omnibus Specification", L.G. Wyndham Shire being the engineer-in-charge.

This rather gorgeous machine was manufactured by Arthur Mulliner of Northampton. Even today Rolls-Royce and other cars of comparative quality are greatly sort after with Mulliner bodies and some of that pure quality has rubbed off on the making of this coach body. The chassis is an AEC Regal powered by a 7.7 litre diesel engine, and the whole vehicle was completed by 10 February 1937.

Detail finish is quite obviously superb, from the front wheel 'dress guards' (which, incidentally, could on other chassis cause brake overheating problems) to the flash on the underskirt which follows its line - almost a piece of sculpture in metal. The oval window at the rear was an odd styling quirk, but the trim continued around under the rear window to make the sides and back a homogeneous whole.

But here's the oddity. In 1938 Duple of Hendon built a facsimile, differing only in minor details - the door handles, the fitting of semaphore signals, wheel trims, seats and underskirt were modified. The chassis used was an elderly Leyland TS2.

Did Duple 'crib' the design or was their version built under licence? We may never know, but let us admire this photograph as an example of British workmanship of the best kind.

At the risk of making a dreadful pun, this photograph leads to a tale of Lions.   The Leyland LT7 chassis was built between 1935 and 1937.   A diesel engine was officially standard, but like many operators Barton chose the 5.1 litre 4-cylinder petrol alternative for their 1937 deliveries.   262 is seen here in pre-war days when fitted with her original rather stylish dual-purpose (bus/coach) 39 seat Duple body.   During the war a greater capacity vehicle was required and as trips to Skegness (for which 262 was purchased) were suspended for the duration a number (probably a dozen) of the Barton 'standards' were sent away to H.V. Burlingham at Blackpool where they were fitted with utility bodies seating 36 but with far greater standing capacity.   Thriftly the old seats and various other fittings were re-used.   In 1949, almost incredibly, new Duple coach-seated bodies replaced the utilities, with oil engines following during 1950!   Versatility in the face of adversity was the name of Barton's game.

Some vehicles lead placid lives and others are true mavericks. Daimler CH6, chassis No. 9030, was first registered as VC 7519 in 1931, fitted with a Birmingham-built Buckingham double deck body, and used as a demonstrator, changing its registration to DH 8638 while with Walsall Corporation but reverting to VC 7519 and carrying No. 100 while with Birmingham Corporation Transport. In 1934 Coventry Corporation hired 'VC', still as No. 100, until 1938 when the sleeve valve petrol engine caught fire in Harnall Lane Garage and the vehicle was burnt out. Returned to Daimler, they found they had no use for a relatively antiquated chassis and sold it to a dealer in June 1939.

Holbrook's were a firm whose penchant lay in the supply of one-off bodies to Midland operators, often on rather obscure chassis, and re-registered (once again!) as DH 8638 and re-bodied the Daimler toured Britain for some years, still being extant in 1952 as an 'ordinary' coach, no longer with Dorothy Holbrook.

Whether Ms Holbrook was a relative of the coachbuilders is not at all clear, but she formed her own band, her 'Harmony Hussars' in 1936. The band was dressed in smart military uniforms with plumed helmets and epaulettes. The band consisted of six accordians, piano, violin, saxophone, trumpet, bass and guitar. They broadcast on Radio Normandy and Radio Luxembourg, and appeared at resorts such as Scarborough, Weston-super-Mare, Minehead, Birkenhead, Caernarfon, and many venues in the Midlands in the late 1930s and 1940s. Married to Leo T. March and mother of two boys she was born in Peterborough and lived in Coventry. Not surprisingly the Daimler was kept in absolutely immaculate condition and the bodywork was of a very attractive design particularly after the 'Early Rectangular' Buckingham body but it is debatable whether it was altogether enhanced by the signwriting.

In earlier days some, perhaps most, councils were very proud of their bus fleets. Caerphilly Urban District Council (Clifford Thomas, Engineer & Manager) was indeed so, and chose, as the forerunner of a new design, this Daimler COG5/40, chassis number 8439 which was fitted with the 1938 show model Willowbrook 39 seat bus body. As can be seen it entered service during the winter of 1938/9 and was to be the forerunner of three more similar machines delivered during 1939. It says much for the vehicles that three more were purchased secondhand from Wolverhampton in 1944, during which year DTX 48 was renovated by Romilly, Cardiff. Further work was carried out, including rubber mounting of windows, by Allens of Bristol in 1948 but No. 33 was rather bedraggled when sold for scrap in April 1955.

Daimler COG 5.

When this drawing was published, 1934, vehicle sales were poor, mainly due to the slump, but also partially as the big companies, having digested many of the small fry during 1932/3 as a consequence of the Road Traffic Acts, had a temporary surfeit of vehicles.

Daimler's strong point, apart from the association with cars chosen by Royalty lay in their unique transmission which "comprises the hydro-dynamic shockless transmission device now well known as the Daimler Fluid Flywheel; a pre-selective, self-changing, silent four- or five-speed gearbox; and the characteristic Daimler worm-driven rear axle. The Daimler Fluid Flywheel has been tested in all conceivable ways - and unanimously approved - by the Daimler testing staff, by independent experts, and by experienced customers of the Daimler Company, during the past four years". The fluid flywheel was 'easily' understood "The drive is transmitted from the engine by means of the interchanges of energy in a rapidly moving fluid, with the result that starting from rest and "take-up" after gear-changing are infinitely smoother than with any other known method of propulsion". Three engine choices existed "(a) Daimler popet-valve, (b) Oil compression-ignition, (c) Daimler sleeve-valve"; chassis types C.P.6, C.O.G. 5, and C.H.6 of which the most popular using the Gardner diesel is illustrated here.

● EARLY DELIVERIES
● STRIP LIGHTING
● FULL LUXURY SEATING
● FITTED RADIO
● "BUILT-IN" RACKS AND HEATING
● MODERN STYLING
● SOUND CONSTRUCTION FOR EASY MAINTENANCE

Luxury Coachwork by

KING & TAYLOR LTD.

GODALMING   SURREY

TELEPHONE
503 (3 LINES)

Immediately after the second world war there was an immense pent-up demand for days-out to anywhere. Few households had cars, even fewer petrol, rationing of basic foodstuffs (meat, butter, sugar, bacon, tea, cheese, confectionary) was not only by the "points" system but also availability. Even into the late 1940s schoolchildren were still being sent home in winter as no coal was available for heating. In 1947 when one of the coldest winters ever was experienced, paraffin - used for both heating and lighting in rural areas - was quite unobtainable. After three or four years of short rations (1943, bacon 8 oz., cheese 2 oz., sugar 8 oz., powdered egg 2 oz., 7 pints of milk were the allotment for two people, not one, per week) it is little wonder that city dwellers were anxious to go out to the countryside where as early as June 1945 strawberries and (real) cream were available. Coach operators, torn between a lack of (rationed) petrol and diesel and a strong desire to make money resurrected vehicles that were laid up in 1939, gazed sadly at the holes from shrapnel or the fungi that flourished on soaking carpets (2'-3' they grew) or gloomily realized that the lean of the body denoted it was rotten through and immediately sought the services of a recognised bodybuilder. But they, too, had problems - design staff were, initially, scarce, materials supply terrible with metals only being alloted if export orders were obtained and many skilled men were not only lost in the war, but lost to other, better paying industries.

However, small companies were advertising promising deliveries in weeks, rather than months or even years. A few were brilliant, many were not. Curiously, two coachbuilding firms operated from Godalming, King & Taylor who in the main bodied Vulcan and Commer chassis but who, despite this advertisement of 1950 had gone shortly afterwards, and Dutfield, one or two of whose bodies remained long enough to enter the preservation era.

During the postwar boom at least half the body builders ostensibly 'in production' commenced their activities prior to 1949 and from this figure of about 40 just two were to survive into 1960. Worse still of the 80 or so British bus and coach builders who advertised their wares prior to 1950, just six remain under there original name today. If one adds those who have re-formed with new capital and a different trade name they can still be counted on both hands.

Most of the companies that fell by the wayside were unable to meet competition, others succumbed because their products were quite unacceptable. King & Taylor for example were advertising a 1930s design twenty years later, while one famous maker designed a fibre glass roofed coach. It leaked and leaked and leaked and defied all attempts to stop the leaks. Another fitted a body to the chassis with just four J-bolts, while their neighbour used aluminium floor joists that literally bounced and within two years were snapping, giving the bodywork rather an Art Deco styling, somewhat wider in the middle than the ends. These firms were doomed. Another cause for concern to firms was the non-delivery of chassis. No problem to re-body existing chassis, even if it meant a bit of fidgeting with the design, but when you have tendered for a contract and the vehicle that arrives is not the one promised two years ago and has anyway been modified in the interim then there are severe difficulties. Churchill Constructors of Norwich bodied this rather jolly Austin CXD for the Royal Arsenal Co-operative Society in 1951. As can be seen the end result was not happy. On this particular chassis, there were difficulties with excessive nose-weight and most machines, including PPG 410, were stripped of their passenger seats forward of the doors, which reduced capacity but left them at least driveable. She was last seen in a breakers' yard, still very smart in 1970 and was presumably scrapped.

Notwithstanding the similarity of TRE 257 to illustration No. 93 these two vehicles began life with quite different object-ives in mind.   New in 1950 SN 388 was ordered and paid for by the Milton Bus Service Limited, one of the Potteries independ-ents, with a Metalcraft 35 seat coach body on a Leyland PS2/3 chassis powered by a Leyland 0.600 engine developing 125 h.p. coupled to a synchromesh gearbox.   A curiosity of Leyland chassis nomenclature is that the code PS2/3 indicated a drop-frame (coach) chassis - PS 2/1 being the bus variant but both were fitted with vacuum brakes.   PS 2/2 and PS 2/4 were reserved for air-braked equivalents which never materialized.

Milton's sold out to Potteries Motor Traction on 1 June 1951 and SN 388 was turned into a bus by the logical over-painting of her trim and flashes (both are still discernible here) and the fitting of an incredibly ugly destination box.   Withdrawn 1963, she was still around in early 1965 but presumably then scrapped.

HL 7510, basking here in the sun at Bakewell, Derbyshire, was a perfectly ordinary traditional bus with nothing really remarkable about her except a life, with only two owners, of 24 years. Built in 1936 her Leyland TS7C chassis was covered with an orthodox 32 seater Roe teak-framed body and the whole delivered to the independent operator, West Riding Automobile Company, in July that year. For many years a style of body had been standardized (if that is the word) by companies within or associated with the British Electric Federation group. Window apertures, wings, entry positions, destination blind layouts and positioning of some interior fittings and lights were all supposed to be alike so that a 'foreign' vehicle could be repaired at any other garage. The outline and window pan sizes were adhered to but with a choice of around 20 chassis from 7 or 8 manufacturers and bodywork being often chosen for political, rather than sensible, reasons (with local employment being ever at the back of the Treasurer's mind) there were many variations upon a theme. The only way HL 7510 differed from many vehicles lay in the "c" after the chassis type as this denoted a "gearless" or torque-converter fitted model; but she had long lost this and gained a standard Leyland gearbox. Useful for ex-tram drivers these converters were very heavy on fuel although the drive along the level roads of, say, Southport, has not been equalled since. The torque converter had no clutch pedal and instead of the normal gear lever there was a control which had four positions - direct, converter, neutral, reverse, with the converter position normally being used from 0 - 20 mph after which direct drive was engaged. The converter acted as an infinitely variable ratio drive but had the major drawback that there was a considerable amount of slip which necessitated large coolers on the side of the chassis to counteract the heat generated by loss of energy. Although here on route 2, HL 7510 worked along The Track to Chesterfield, as much as she roared up the bank from Bakewell via Shutts Lane. Youlgrave always found any missed maintenance, while Hartington could load her better than ever Wakefield did: 32 seats she had, but with an 8.6 litre diesel engine a standing mob could be accommodated and rarely, if ever, were passengers left behind. Withdrawn 1960 and presumably scrapped.

The Commercial Motor Show held at Earls Court, London, in 1952 was probably the last time when a number of manufacturers of bodies and chassis were able to exhibit but for just ten days from 26 September we could gaze upon visions of the future. Some were beautiful designs and long lived, others weird and ephemeral, but - and here's the rub - to look down the catalogue is to see Britain's PSV manufacturing industry, much of it Midland based, and all now history. And it's such a sadness and a waste of men's skills that somewhere, somehow over the last forty years we've thrown it all away.

This particular machine depicts a Burlingham "Seagull" Mark II Coach body on a Daimler Freeline chassis type D65OHS, like Yeates, Maudslay and AEC, who are mentioned on page 95, Burlingham and Daimler are no longer a part of the PCV manufacturing industry.

94

In 1952 W.A. Yeates of Loughborough used the AEC/Maudslay Mk IV as the basis for their 39 seater 'Riviera' Touring Coach. The body was ultra-modern in style, perhaps too much so for our conservative operators who in the main were still wondering where the radiator had gone. Yeates had started building new bodies in 1945, and produced many ingenious and often flamboyant designs before ceasing manufacture in 1963, having built 1011 new passenger vehicles in that time.

Curiously the Maudslay Regal Mk IV chassis only offered the 4-speed and reverse synchromesh box which met with some driver resistance. The AEC alternative was a fluid flywheel plus an air operated pre-selective 4-speed box, with 'easy-use' column mounted gear lever. At least one Mk IV was anachronistically fitted with an old-fashioned crash box and its arrival at the Coliseum, Blackpool, after the run from Coventry was regarded by other drivers as a minor side-show to the lights, particularly when crunched by a part-time driver.

The Maudslay Motor Company of Alcester, Warwickshire, had lost their independence as a manufacturer in 1948 when they became a member of the ACV group, of which the other main constituents were AEC of London and Crossley Motors of Errwood, Lancashire. They were to become a parts-only producer and such was then the pressure upon floor space at the Commercial Motor Show that each company was only allocated one stand. But by adapting the regulations ACV were able to take three stands as three separate companies so that just briefly this Midland company could show whole vehicles, albeit 'badge engineered'.

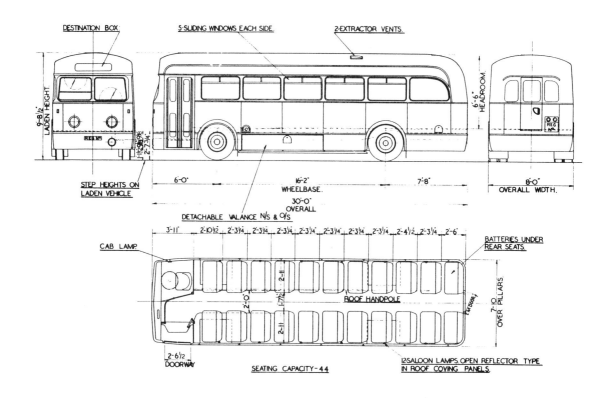

DESTINATION BOX

5 SLIDING WINDOWS EACH SIDE.

2 EXTRACTOR VENTS.

9'-8½" LADEN HEIGHT

6'-6" HEADROOM

STEP HEIGHTS ON LADEN VEHICLE

6'-0"

16'-2" WHEELBASE

7'-8"

30'-0" OVERALL

8'-0" OVERALL WIDTH.

DETACHABLE VALANCE N/S & O/S

3'-11" 2'-10½" 2'-3¼" 2'-3¼" 2'-3¼" 2'-3¼" 2'-3¼" 2'-3¼" 2'-3¼" 2'-4½" 2'-3¼" 2'-6"

CAB LAMP

BATTERIES UNDER REAR SEATS.

ROOF HANDPOLE

7'-10 OVER PILLARS

2'-6½" DOORWAY

SEATING CAPACITY - 44

12 SALOON LAMPS OPEN REFLECTOR TYPE IN ROOF COVING PANELS.

"HERMES"

MCW.	LIGHTWEIGHT SINGLE DECK BUS ON LEYLAND "TIGER CUB" CHASSIS.	DESIGN No. V2716

The Metropolitan-Cammell-Weymann "Hermes" was one of a new generation of lightweight bodies. Introduced in 1952, MCW kept the weight of a 44 seat bus down to 36 cwt. (1832 kg) while providing a reasonably robust, almost corrosion free vehicle of modern design. Within the North Western Road Car fleet Leyland Tiger Cub chassis with Weymann (M.C.W.) "Hermes" bodywork totalled 132 out of nearly 600 vehicles during the 1950s and it is therefore fitting that we have not only a photograph of one en route from Ashbourne to Buxton, number 562A having entered service in 1954, but also plan drawings, so that unusually some indication of what lay 'under the skin' of an ordinary service bus can be ascertained.

Photo - R.H.G. Simpson

The Torpoint Ferry, depicted here in 1952 was first recorded as operating in 1791 but the 'new' chain ferry steam bridges, replacing those of 1871 and 1878, entered service in 1925 and 1926. Each could carry around 800 people and 26 'average sized' cars, but the Duple bodied Bedford OB belonging to Marigold Coaches and (just discernable behind the lorry) a Duple bodied SB plus the lorry only left room for at best a dozen. The OB's destination is shown as Lanner, around 60 miles from the Ferry.

To the bystander the increase in permitted maximum dimensions of PSVs has been almost imperceptible as for years all sizes jostled together on the roads. The operator, obviously, greatly favoured length increases as the ratio of paying heads to drivers' wages rose in his favour - a modest 2' 6" (76 cm) enlargement meant four more seats.

Width was different and although 2.5m (8' 2¼") is now the norm there remains a strong market for sub 7' 6" vehicles for use around lanes. When in 1950 the permitted width changed from 7' 6" (2.286m) to 8' 0" (2.438m) operators were able to increase seat and gangway widths usually by 1½" (38mm) and 3" respectively but there was a price to pay. East Kent FFN 453 was a Park Royal centre-entrance coach with 37 seats on Leyland Royal Tiger heavyweight underfloor engined chassis. She was built to the new 8' 0" width in 1951, and was sent off to Calais to test the loading and unloading arrangements on the Cross-Channel ferry. Today we nonchalantly drive on and off without a care; the 1951 problem is self-evident from the photograph.

The M & D and East Kent Bus Club

This could almost be described as a diabolical liberty. The chassis of 6876 RE is an air-braked Bedford SB8, powered by a Leyland 5.76 litre 0.350 diesel engine and the body a perfectly normal Duple 41 seater. But the destination box is the most ghastly disfigurement ever added to a normal rather svelte coach outline. New in 1960, she came to P.M.T. when the firm of Staniers Limited of Newchapel were acquired in 1965 and was given the fleet number SL 997. Withdrawn in 1968, she went to a dealer, but was later used by a Scots operator for a few years.

A superb example of a clean design was this Duple of Hendon bodied AEC Regal delivered new to the Bristol Tramways & Carriage Company in February 1938. No. 2095 in their fleet, only the slightly out-of-keeping blind apertures detract from one of the simplest, quietly elegant styles of bodywork to be found in the 1930s, when flamboyance was the mode of the day.

Seating 32 passengers when delivered, she was 'called up' in 1939 and ended on loan to London Transport from June 1940 to August 1941, being gutted of her coach seats and with bus seating installed, thus accommodating at least 40. After her service in the capital a plaque was fitted to the front bulkhead to remind passengers how cities could work together when necessity required it. Refitted in 1945 the bodywork was tired and strained so she had to be withdrawn in 1951 when Duple body No. 2041 was scrapped but the chassis was dismantled and partially re-used.

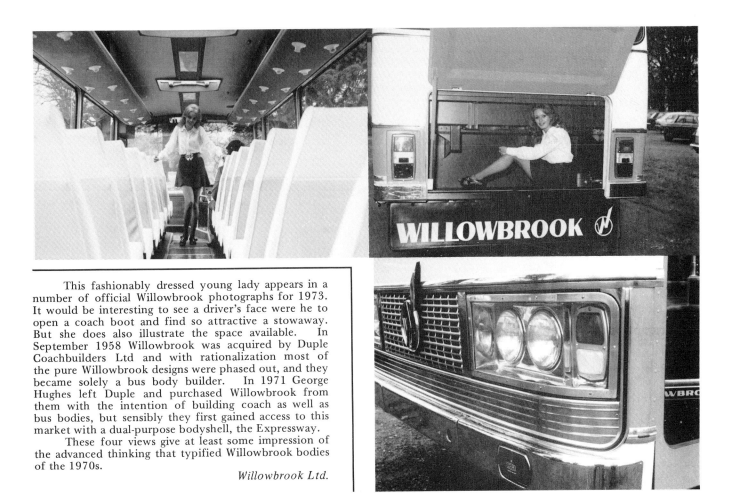

This fashionably dressed young lady appears in a number of official Willowbrook photographs for 1973. It would be interesting to see a driver's face were he to open a coach boot and find so attractive a stowaway. But she does also illustrate the space available. In September 1958 Willowbrook was acquired by Duple Coachbuilders Ltd and with rationalization most of the pure Willowbrook designs were phased out, and they became solely a bus body builder. In 1971 George Hughes left Duple and purchased Willowbrook from them with the intention of building coach as well as bus bodies, but sensibly they first gained access to this market with a dual-purpose bodyshell, the Expressway.

These four views give at least some impression of the advanced thinking that typified Willowbrook bodies of the 1970s.

Willowbrook Ltd.

From 16 July 1947, the London Passenger Transport Board was chosen by British European Airways to provide, under contract, services from various London termini to Northolt and, later, London Airport (Heathrow). Initially the service was provided by Park Royal bodied Commer Commando chassis, Bedford OB with Duple and S.M.T. bodies, and Spurling bodied Bedford KZ. From 1952 AEC Regal IV with Park Royal special bodies replaced most of these but after a number of experiments including use of an AEC Regent V and a 'special' RMF, the Regals were in turn replaced by 65 Routemasters fitted with folding doors immediately behind the engine instead of being rear-loaders.

To get round the problem of luggage (at the time 20kg was allowed for Tourist Class passengers and 30kg for First/Executive) by special authority of the Ministry of Transport, these Routemasters were allowed to tow a two-wheeled baggage trailer. Normally, for safety reasons, PSVs were not allowed to tow trailers but to put the luggage into a front-loader RM would not only be physically difficult, but inordinately wasteful on space. Eventually (to allow for loading and Customs) 88 trailers were ordered from Marshalls of Cambridge.

The first batches of these 'special' RMs were delivered in 1966, and the balance, including NMY 629E seen here, arrived a year later. Although the RMs were satisfactory in service, the trailers were not entirely so and 70 replacements arrived in August 1972 from Locomotors, Mitcham, after which they remained more or less permanently attached to their 'host' Routemasters. For various reasons these airport RMs were to become superfluous in the mid-1970s and classified 'RMA' a few entered normal London Transport service, but were disapproved of by the Trade Unions. Some were, however, to find their own niche in the 1980s as sightseeing vehicles.

This superb Harrington of Hove bodied AEC Reliance, seen when still new in 1964 has all the combination of elegance and thrust that typified British products in their heyday. Fleet number 0420F within the British Overseas Airways fleet, she was based at Prestwick, then commonly used as an aerodrome for uplifting and setting down passengers to and from New York. After ten years work for B.O.A.C. between Prestwick and Glasgow (this is St. Enoch Station) 0420F and her sister were transferred to British Airways and downgraded within the 'European Division' as non-P.S.V. shuttle-buses, being withdrawn a year later. AAG 651B was subsequently rebodied and re-registered NGP 172P.

R.H.G. Simpson

The courtesy coach is a very vital aspect of PSV operation that is often overlooked. The Ariel Hotel was one of the first 'super' hotels to be built near London Airport Central, (now Heathrow) and they ordered and had operated on their behalf this Bedford J2SZ10 with a Plaxton 14 seat Embassy body. Of, normally, a 20 seat design, a luggage pen supplementing the quite large boot replaced the rear five seats, and the courier (single) seat at the front was not used by passengers. Basically a normal control (bonnetted) tipper chassis, these vehicles have quite a pleasant ride, are unbelievably economic with a four cylinder diesel engine, and until the cessation of commerical vehicle manufacture by Bedford, easily obtainable spares. Speeds of 50+ mph are easily attained, albeit the noise level from the engine becomes horrendous, and while here wheeltrims are in situ, these tended to be easily 'lost' as those well shrouded brakes overheat in heavy traffic. But what a beautiful machine ONK was!

Plaxtons (Scarborough) Ltd.

If the BEA Routemaster exemplified dignity then this little Bedford must represent coaching impudence. Seen here in the colours of its 1992 owners, Hillcrest Radio Coaches, RNE 693W, a Bedford CF350 with Plaxton MiniSupreme bodywork, began her PSV service as part of the Shearings Holidays fleet, where her duties involved ferrying passengers and aircrew to Manchester Airport, inter airport transfer duties and uplifting passengers from the Airport to their tour coaches. With a 17-seater capacity, like the J2 of the Ariel Hotel, top speed is inhibited by noise, and in the case of RNE the original diesel has been replaced by the standard 2.3 litre low compression petrol engine. Plaxton's are uncertain how many of these were built, although the number probably did not exceed 40, the price of such scaled down 'real' coaches has led to their replacement by conversions of normal commercial vans.

It may read like a fable today but once upon a time in the 1950s during the rush-hour Britain's buses could not uplift passengers fast enough. The normal 30' x 8' bus seated around 39 with between 5 and 12 passengers allowed to stand. There was also two crew, the driver and the conductor, giving a ratio of 20:1 passengers to staff which vexed the management who thereupon sought methods of improving this. One answer was less seats and more standing passengers, a chimera of efficiency that has been sought since forever. The Bristol LWL was available between 1951 and 1954 and this Eastern Coach Works body was one of a batch downseated and fitted with a wide circulating area. By so doing Western National were able to alter the normal 39 seats + 8 standing arrangement to one of 31 seats plus 15 standing, which while not increasing its capacity allowed a far faster turnover of passengers and better time-keeping, which again aided efficiency. A curious side effect was that the cleaners were able to get around the floor far faster and thus handle more vehicles per shift. The combined match strikers/cigarette stubbers are prominent and then most desirable.

The boldest attempt at operating routes with 'standee' driver-only vehicles was that carried out in London. In 1964, London Transport advised a Government Committee that it wished to experiment with 'standee' buses in Central London, carrying passengers for relatively short journeys. Initially flat fare operations would involve eliminating the conductor, but multi-stage trips would still require a two-person crew. The first flat fare (6d - 2½p) vehicles measured 36' long (11m) and were designed to carry 75 passengers, of whom 50 stood, entered service on 18 April 1966 on a limited-stop service from Victoria via Hyde Park to Marble Arch. They were successful to the extent that in September 1966 LT decided that they would accept over 600 AEC 'Merlin' rear engined vehicles with the intention that one-person operated single deckers would replace Routemasters almost throughout the system. Eventually 665 were built. Problems arose (mainly due to physical weaknesses) in these 'MB' class vehicles, and a new design the SM (Short Merlin) at 33' 5" (10m) was chosen for later orders. These 'Swift' machines had 33 seats and carried 34 standing within their mainly Park Royal or MCW built bodies. This is SMS (Short Merlin Standee) 834, the fifth from last to be built, and delivered in 1971. In 1973 the replacement of the whole Merlin fleet was agreed, the Swifts following from 1976; all bar a handful of the 1503 Merlin/Swift family had gone from London Transport by 1985.

John Fozard

IRISH INTERLUDE

6237 EZ is a coach with a difference. The chassis is a Southall-built AEC Reliance but the forty bodies for this batch of vehicles (6234-6273) were built by the Ulster Transport Authorities' engineering workshop in Duncrue Street, Belfast in 1963 to a refreshingly different design. Fortunately 6234 has been preserved and is a magnificent sight in her two tone blue livery.

R.C. Ludgate

Northern Ireland is, of course, a part of the United Kingdom and has been intensely loyal in their purchasing of Public Service Vehicles. For a number of reasons transport is almost entirely in the hands of two separate bodies, Ulsterbus and [Belfast] Citybus. Leyland B21 No.1. 3004 (WO1 3004) with Alexander (Belfast) 33 seat bodywork is seen working service 25 City Centre-Holywood Road (near Gilbert Bridge) when new in 1982.

R.C. Ludgate

The chassis of the coach is a normal Volvo B10M but the body was an attempt by Duple Coachbuilders Ltd to break away from the supposed constraints of orthodox coach designs.

It has been suggested that giving this slightly unorthodox model the type name "Dominant III" may have confused the market as Domi I, II and IV had, at least, 'normal' windows. The straightforward Dominant I first appeared in 1972 and was available on chassis from the 29 seat Bedford VAS to the largest 12 metre 53 seaters. The Domi II, an updated variant was first shown in 1976, and the III and IV both appeared in 1980. The principle behind the sloping, small, darkened windows of the Domi III was that a passenger on long motorway runs has no interest in the outside scenery and would prefer a video. Double glazing ensured a relatively silent ride.

But the high waistrail and the darkened glass was found to give some passengers claustrophobic feelings and a degree of resistance was found by operators. The contrast with any of the recent 'ordinary' bodies in this book is quite marked, the Alexander Y body was a mild version with much larger slanted windows, but remarkably airy inside.

The classical coach of the 1970s and one that remains in service today, albeit in dwindling numbers, was the Leyland Leopard chassis in one of its guises, clothed by the Duple Dominant bodyshell.   One of the problems with the 'Domi' is that its very success has led to the school/service bus/outings coach syndrome where the similarity leads passengers to regard them all as being alike; being unable to distinguish between, say, a Ford/Domi or Bristol/Domi.   Seating 49 passengers in, if not luxury, reasonable comfort NNN2M was one of a batch of four Leyland Leopard PSU3 Dominant I coaches that entered the fleet of East Midlands Motor Services in 1974.   Together with the 1976 introduced Dominant II, Duple Coachbuilders Ltd found that in the late 1970s production was running at over 1000 per annum.

The AEC Reliance chassis was first placed in service in 1953 powered by a 7¾ litre engine. Its predecessor, the Regal IV, the first true underfloor engined chassis from AEC, was a real heavyweight with (relatively) poor fuel consumption, but not unsurprisingly was magnificently strong. The Reliance was classed as a medium weight chassis and for a while had a mixed reputation. In certain circumstances the cooling system could give problems, but AEC were well aware of this and offered various remedial packages to such an extent that one of the original chassis remained in commercial service unti a couple of years ago. Engine power increased until in the chassis classification 8U2R shown the AH 691 design of 11.3 litres rated at 157 b.h.p. at 2,000 r.p.m. is to be found. Transmission for the 8U2R is by way of a semi-automatic electro-mechanically controlled 5-speed box, to a fully floating spiral bevel axle. Brakes are Girling cam-operated leading shoes on 15½″ (40 cm) diameter drums, with separate air circuits to each axle. The Reliance was (and is) a very economic vehicle, and even when fitted with the Alexander 49 seat semi-coach body seen here, despite weighing 12 tons 6 cwt. (12,500 kg.) fully laden could turn in 17 m.p.g. when cruising and rarely gave below 10 m.p.g. Speed at the time of this illustration, 1967, was a little academic but 65 m.p.h. (105 kph) was attainable, assisted by the unique suspension of the 8U series, coil springs replacing air bellows. KVT 195E, Potteries Motor Traction 1095 had chassis No. 8U2R 6735 and entered service in 1967.

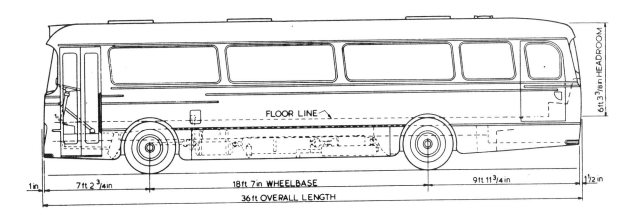

6ft 3³/₈ in HEADROOM

FLOOR LINE

1 in   7ft 2³/₄ in   18ft 7in WHEELBASE   9ft 11³/₄ in   1¹/₂ in

36ft OVERALL LENGTH

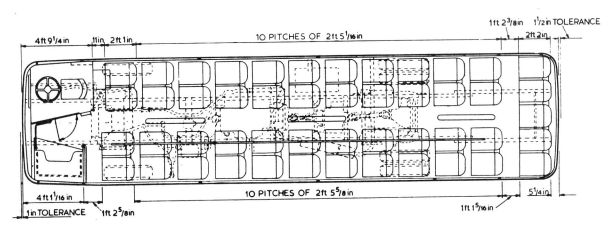

1ft 2³/₈ in   1¹/₂ in TOLERANCE

4ft 9¹/₄ in   11in   2ft 1 in   10 PITCHES OF 2ft 5¹/₁₆ in   2ft 2in

10 PITCHES OF 2ft 5⁵/₈ in   5¹/₄ in

4ft 1¹/₁₆ in   1ft 1⁵/₁₆ in

1 in TOLERANCE   1ft 2⁵/₈ in

The Duple 'Vega' coach body made its appearance at the 1950 Commercial Motor Show mounted on and purposely built for the Bedford SB chassis. The primary objective of this combination was to produce a successor to the Bedford OB/Duple products of the 1940s. They were to be incredibly successful, the SB chassis, in various guises, remaining in production until December 1986 when General Motors (of the USA) decreed Bedford lorry and coach productions should cease, while the Vega, Bella Vega, Bella Venture and Bella Vista bodies all having some (albeit remote) family connection were available until 1970. TXJ 709 shows the 'Classic' outline familiar to many passengers, it is not inapposite for such a coach to be shown in close juxtaposition to a public house!

In *Passenger Transport* 13 May 1953 C.R. Robson of Hexham expressed his delight in his new 'Vega'.

"I have much pleasure in writing to you regarding my new 'Vega' Passenger Coach. It is really a masterpiece in performance considering the seating capacity. It can take such hills as the Kirkstone Pass with a full load with ease, and passengers never fail to appreciate the beautiful riding qualities of the coach. The extra wide seats of the Duple coachwork give that luxury and restful feeling when they do not wish to leave the coach at the end of a journey. Petrol consumption, with a full load is just under ten miles to the gallon on these North Country roads, and 10½ to 11 miles to the gallon on level roads".

NATIONAL-IZED

Arguments over the success or otherwise of the Leyland National will last as long as the vehicles. In terms of sales numbers it was probably the most successful single bus design ever, but whether its existence accelerated the decline in passenger loads or whether this would have happened anyway even if the Bristol RE and similar vehicles had been thoroughly developed we shall never know.

At its simplest when first shown in 1970, the National was to be a highly standardized, integrally constructed city bus. Nothing more, nothing less. A new highly sophisticated factory with a production capacity of 2000 units (primarily buses) per year was built at Workington, Cumberland, where unemployment was rife, but engineering skills almost unknown.

Two lengths were offered and one engine, the infamous 'headless wonder', a fixed head Leyland 510 turbocharged diesel. No Gardner, no easy-to-work-on Leyland 600 or 680.

Instead of 2000 buses per annum, mechanical problems and people-resistance kept production down to a total of 6500 Mk 1 models between 1972 and 1979, when the Mark II with, at last, a decent engine, commenced manufacture. By 1982, Leyland were forced to re-design the National to take the Gardner engine, but this was too late the last Mk. II rolling out of Workington in November 1985. In 1987 Leyland was privatized and sold to its management but just over 12 months later was resold to Volvo.

P.C., D.W. & A.S. Ludlow of Halesowen have owned quite a choice collection of Nationals, mostly carrying their famous Black Country dialect phrase "Buzz with uz". RFM 886M is a 49-seater ex-Crosville (SNL 886) in 1987, shown in both 1988 and 1991 liveries.

Gideon Graphics

By and large buses and coaches are regarded as inanimate collections of steel, glass, rubber, wood plastic and seat covering materials. Conversely some enthusiasts point out the workmanship that went into many vehicles and claim this gives them a form of life, if not a soul. Whatever the truth of it no-one could deny these three Nationals appear to be huddling together, perhaps in the knowledge that the old bus station in Worcester, was shortly to be demolished when this March 1992 photograph was taken. JOX 509P, NOE 539 and 540R are standard Nationals, 49 seaters (chassis type 11351) delivered 1975-7.

BVP 809V is a Leyland National Mk.II of 1980, (chassis classification 2 NL116L11/1R), and when seen here 29 March 1980, No. 809 in the Midland Red fleet, itself a part of the nationalized National Bus Company. In 1988 BVP 809V passed from Midland Red (North) to the North Western fleet, as No. 273. Rickerscote is a village approximately 1¾ miles south of Stafford.

P.R. Gainsbury

NATIONALLY EXPRESSED

During the era of state ownership what more logical than to call the nationalized coaching arm of the National Bus Company "National Express"?   The illogic lay in subsidizing both rail and coach to run on parallel routes.   The NBC was formed on 28 November 1968, and within a year they were employing in excess of 81,000 staff and operating 21,000 vehicles. The first 'National' coach timetable is that of summer 1973 with 'National Express' becoming a publicly recognised brand name within a year or so.

The return of a courier to coaches in 1981 was hailed as a great advance, although commonplace in the 1920s and 1930s. As then on-board refreshments became available, together with a toilet and such 'Rapide' services undoubtedly reduced travelling time by the elimination of comfort stops.   Aided by road and vehicle improvements we find that London-Penzance in 1973 required 13 hours but in 1985 had come down to 6¾ hours on the 'Rapide' service, albeit the orthodox route 700 still required 9¾ hours.   However, to show how timings had stagnated prior to the NBC one must add that in 1951 Royal Blue took 13 hours 36 minutes with eight comfort stops!

National Express was privatized (through a management buy-out) on 17 March 1988, but have subsequently changed hands and are now only an operating company, hiring in the 700 or so vehicles required for their 90,000,000 miles run each year.   Vehicle types are theoretically strictly regulated but when traffic demands it, some variety may be found.

KAD 357V is an older vehicle than most of those found in National colours and is included to show a completely different livery.   The vehicle itself is a Leyland Leopard PSU5C/4R which, while an up-to-date chassis when delivered to Wessex National in 1980, is rather less than usual fare on express work in 1993.   The body style represents the Plaxton Supreme IV, of which many examples remain in service today.   Yardley Coaches, the owners, operate one of the longest National Express routes, the 547 Edinburgh-Penzance.

A 212 SAE is a 1983 vehicle and therefore theoretically outside the 7-year age limit normally expected from National Express contractors, but was still in service during 1992. Undeniably her Plaxton Paramount bodywork is immaculate both inside and out and she is a credit to her owners, the Cheltenham & Gloucester Omnibus Company who operate route 712 London to Hereford and Gloucester. The 'Welcome Aboard' sign, if a little hackneyed, is often reflected by the driver's greetings.

J310 REL, photographed in Leicester on a miserably cold mid-summer day has a Volvo B10M-60 chassis, with a 49 seat-plus-toilet Plaxton Expressliner body.   At the time of the photograph it was the latest vehicle in the fleet of Sea View Coaches (Poole)Ltd., and operating on route 310 Bradford-Poole. Coming up behind is a Leyland Tiger with Plaxton bodywork, J8 DLT, from the touring fleet of Dunn-Line of Nottingham and on hire to National Express, albeit on a trip basis only. Although basically identically styled machines, the Dunn-Line vehicle is noticeably lower than J310 REL.

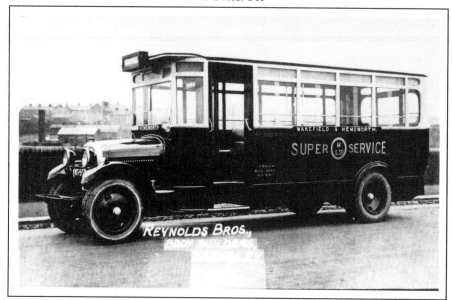

During the 1920s and 1930s many of the small homely bodybuilders who would turn out a bespoke bus or coach body for the local operator often found they could no longer compete with the big firms in the business particularly as their 'early rectangular' designs had required little in the way of drawing office skills, and as long as Sid or Fred was gainfully employed repairing Major Smith's Rolls Royce, Mr. Brown's hearse or Farmer Giles' carts then they could ease this work in between 'main' jobs. The joinery involved was relatively simple although the canvas roofs of some models seemed to call more for sailors' skills and while "safety glass" was used (and boasted about) for the windscreens, ordinary ¼" plate was still to be found elsewhere even in the 1950s. As late as 1947 one small (and shortly to be defunct) firm bedded bus windows in with putty!

However, because the old arts of coachbuilding and coachpainting had not been lost in a purely pecuniary world the actual structure and the finished paint jobs were as good as any done on Major Smith's Rolls.

Some degree of styling was axiomatic as firms of this type appreciated a good 'line' even if their equipment was insufficently sophisticated to allow them to survive when elaborate curves and swirls became the vogue.

This little beauty was built by Reynolds Brothers of Barnsley on one of the lightweight chassis of the 1920s, the G.M.C. Fred Masson of Mount Avenue, Hemsworth (8¼ miles from Wakefield) was the recipient with the vehicle costing £300 or so.

Fred Masson's little bus held 20 passengers and so qualified for conductor-less operation. In the last decade driver-only minibuses have been quite in vogue. Carlyle Bus Centre Ltd., once the Carlyle Works of BMMO, rather specialized in these, leasing them out at quite reasonable rates. These are Freight Rover based 20-seater vehicles seen in mid-1992 after the closure of Carlyle and the dispersal of their stock.

Alan Wilson (PSV) Ltd., of Ratby had these two for sale around the same time. The 1986 Renault (12 seats + courier) was described as a "luxury mini coach" and had a "hot drinks machine, radio and stereo cassette", while the 1984 Mercedes was fitted with "12 high back moquette seats" and was "available from stock".

To present the 1992 face of coaching two vehicles from the fleet of J.W. Carnell, Sutton Bridge, Spalding, Linconshire will serve excellently. In 1990, Carnells had 25 vehicles in service, varying from the oldest, a 1974 Plaxton bodied Bedford, to the then latest, a 1988 Mercedes-Benz Reeves Burgess 18 seater. The fleet was interestingly varied, from a 12 seat Ford Transit to a 57 seat Bedford, although the majority of the coaches seated 53. Chassis makers included, other than the above, AEC, Leyland, Volvo and DAF.

B500 SJL is a magnificent blue and white Duple 53-seat body on a Bedford YNT chassis and was built in 1984 while B290 TCT has a high floor 1983 Duple 55 seat body but on a DAF chassis and looked absolutely superb in white with red and gold stripes, the latter rather lost in reproduction. Their yard was also enhanced by flower beds, which softens the necessarily workaday appearance of any coaching depot.

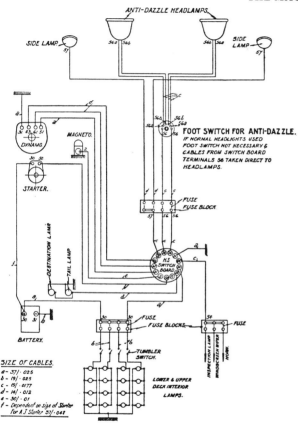

ANTI-DAZZLE HEADLAMPS.

SIDE LAMP.

SIDE LAMP.

MAGNETO.

DYNAMO.

STARTER.

FOOT SWITCH FOR ANTI-DAZZLE.

IF NORMAL HEADLIGHTS USED
FOOT SWITCH NOT NECESSARY &
CABLES FROM SWITCH BOARD
TERMINALS 56 TAKEN DIRECT TO
HEADLAMPS.

FUSE
FUSE BLOCK

H.S
SWITCH
BOARD

DESTINATION LAMP

TAIL LAMP

FUSE
FUSE BLOCKS

FUSE

BATTERY.

TUMBLER
SWITCH.

INSPECTION LAMP
WINDSCREEN WIPER
HORN.

LOWER & UPPER
DECK INTERIOR
LAMPS.

SIZE OF CABLES.
a - 37/·025
b - 19/·025
c - 19/·0177
d - 14/·012
e - 30/·...
f - Dependent on size of Starter
for A J Starter 37/·048

*General wiring diagram of the Bosch C.T. dynamo and switch-board for
covered-top double-deck buses.*

STARTERS FOR BUS ENGINES

There is a growing tendency to install electric motors for
starting the engines of modern omnibuses. It is not intended here
to discuss the merits and the petrol economy to be gained by install-
ing a starter, neither is it proposed to refer to the types of starters
commonly used. As the great majority of omnibuses operating today are not fitted with an electric starter, it is frequently asked how
to determine the size of an electric starter for a given engine. The
type of electric motor used is called a series motor; that is to say,
the field winding is in series with the armature winding. This class
of motor is chosen chiefly because it develops its maximum torque
at zero speed, and is always operated with load. Where a dynamometer or spring balance is available, the size of starter can be
accurately determined. It is seldom, however, that such instru-
ments are available, nevertheless the size of starter can with reasonable accuracy be calculated by empirical formulæ.

ASCERTAINING STARTING TORQUE BY DYNAMOMETER

If a nynamometer is available, connect it to the starting
handle of the engine. Then pull at the handle of the dynamometer
until the piston goes over compression, and note the maximum
reading in pounds or kilograms. Do this for about six times, note
the reading each time, and take the average. Then measure the
length of the starting handle - centre of crankshaft to centre of
handle to which the dynamometer is attached. Multiply the average
pull in pounds or kilograms by the length of the arm in feet or
metres and the figure so obtained will be the torque required to turn
the engine in lbs., ft. or mt.kg., depending on the units used. As
starting is hardest when the lubricating oil is cold, this test should
be made under the lowest temperature conditions at which the
engine will ever be required to start.

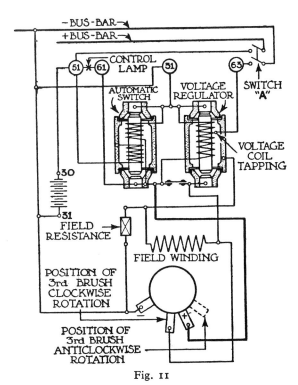

Fig. 11

Internal wiring diagram of the Bosch C.T. dynamo for covered-top double-deck buses.

In 1927 the fitting of a dynamo represented modernity. Competition was fierce; each make claimed to be more versatile than the other.

. . . . . *"The diagram shows the internal wiring diagram of the C.T. dynamo for covered-top double-deck buses. It will be noticed that this dynamo is fitted with a third brush, as well as a regulator and cut-out, and had four terminals.*

That marked 51 is the positive terminal; 61 is the control lamp terminal, and 31 is the negative terminal.

Terminal 63 has a special function in that the dynamo will generate two tensions depending whether the switch "A" is "opened" or "closed" - a higher tension when "open" and a lower tension when "closed". It will be observed that switch "A" is linked to be operated with the main lighting switch, the reason for this being to make it impossible to close the lighting switch in advance of the switch connecting terminal 63, thus preventing a high voltage being applied to the bulbs.

When using a ten-cell Alklum, or Nife battery, or a 9-cell Edison battery, two tensions are required, a higher tension to ensure the battery being properly charged, and a lower tension to prevent the over-stressing of the lamp bulbs.

For bus services where the daylight running is of such short periods that it is found the nine-cell nickel iron batteries require an occasional boost, terminal 63 could be used with great advantage. That is to say, instead of permanently connecting this terminal to the negative bus bar a switch could be inserted which normally would be closed. To get a boosting charge to the battery this switch could be "opened" for a certain period during daylight running, but this should be done only under strict supervision of the foreman.

It will also be noted that for day running of the bus the voltage of the dynamo is such as fully to charge the battery, whether of the lead-acid or nickel-iron type, and that with the switching on of the lamps the voltage is reduced, ensuring that the filaments are not overstressed". . . . . .

129

Until the relatively recent advent of reliable alternators, virtually all motor vehicles relied upon the humble dynamo. Curious things could happen to dynamos as the voltage regulator could send a message that the battery was flat and within minutes the battery would be virtually boiling and the headlights dazzling. Neither lasted long. The carbon brush on a dynamo could lose its temper and make performance erratic. After an hour or so the battery being virtually discharged would show its displeasure and the engine begin to hunt; a rapid switching off of all main lights, heater fan (if fitted) and any other electrical equipment might get you home.

But the biggest problem with a dynamo was its output. It was always reckoned that to recharge a battery after one start in the morning took a car dynamo nine miles (14 km) of constant (30 mph) driving. Buses and coaches obviously had different requirements and the only way to meet these was by altering the drive ratios for which empirical diagrams existed. The ideal charging rate was 40 amperes at a dynamo speed of 1000 r.p.m. For a Leyland petrol engine of 6.8 litres the gearing was established as being 1½:1 - a maximum engine speed of 2250 r.p.m. equalled a dynamo speed of 3400 r.p.m. - around its peak output. For this example the presumption was that the bus would cruise at between 9.6 m.p.h. and 36 m.p.h.

For a Daimler city bus, where speeds were lower, between 6 and 10 m.p.h. for at least 65% of its working day, a ratio of 1¾:1 geared the dynamo up to give its 40 ampere rate at the lower speed.

For a Dennis country bus it was assumed that 70% of its time the vehicle would run between 15 and 30 m.p.h. so a direct 1:1 ratio would suffice.

A 'BRIGHTER' SERVICE

You can always rely on Siemens Lamps to give you the best possible service under the most arduous conditions. Bright, steady illumination to ensure passenger comfort, plus a long life are compelling reasons why you should always specify Siemens Lamps for your coaches and buses.

SIEMENS LAMPS

Obviously there has to be progress. At its simplest contrast the old constant-mesh (crash) gearbox still in common use in the 1960s with, thirty years later, the computer assisted gearbox. The older box was brutally mechanical, and almost indestructable. When it was worn any half-way competent mechanic could carry out repairs. Today's boxes rely on electronics and the average mechanic of those days might at first sight have found a course of black magic would help him understand the gizmos involved. And so it is with all the electrics of a PSV. The wiring diagram relates to a 1927 double decker and is easy to comprehend. Even the instructions on fitting a starter are relatively simple. The Lucas-C.A.V. 551 Transmission Controller represents today's 'state of the art'. It is a superb piece of electronics and one which drivers of 1927 could only dream of; the delicacy one can use on the 'loud pedal' together with ease of gear selection compensate to some extent for the less attractive traffic conditions.

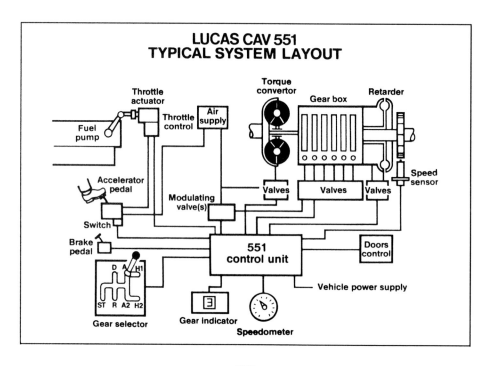

GENERAL DESCRIPTION AND OPERATION OF SYSTEM

The CAV transmission control system incorporating the 551 microprocessor control unit provides for either fully automatic or protected semi-automatic modes of operation. Apart from the benefit of smooth gear changes an even greater advantage is the reduction of wear in the gearbox and drive train allowing a corresponding increase in service life.

The 551 system incorporates a speed signal generator consisting of a multi-toothed wheel or annulus which is driven by the gearbox at a speed proportional to road speed irrespective of the gear engaged together with an electromagnetic transducer. A signal proportional to road speed is therefore passed to the control board.

Standard features of the control board are the infinitely and independantly variable gear delays, throttle dip delays and throttle dip times available on all up and down gear changes. Pressure modulation is an optional feature that can be made available during gear changes or at other specified times.

A door inter-lock facility may be incorporated which can be programmed in a variety of ways to suit individual customer requirements.

Retarder controls can be included to give various selectable switched inputs and output stages which may be speed or gear-engaged dependant. A transmission safety over-ride (T.S.O.) is also present which may sense either air pressure gearbox oil temperature, oil pressure or oil flow, and which can be used to partially or fully disable retarders or prevent upshifts above a certain gear or even completely immobilize a vehicle under certain conditions. A speedometer drive output signal is available on all 551 control boards. A forward-reverse interlock is incorporated to prevent directional changes being achieved before the vehicle comes to rest.

The program can incorporate a maximum overpseed limit to inhibit engine overspeed by introducing a throttle dip and activating the retarder to prevent engine or transmission damage. Many applications have permanent throttle dip in neutral which prevents a gear being selected while the engine is above idling.

It will be appreciated that because of the flexibility and versatility of the control parameters it is essential that persons involved with vehicle transmission control systems are fully conversant with the requirements of their own particular applications.

Lucas Electrical Systems - Heavy Duty

Naval brass on steel worm gear reduces wear and extends life.

You can count on it

If your hubodometer doesn't provide an extremely accurate count of miles traveled, your losing money.
hubodometers are indispensable tools for increasing your profitability. They're important for:
• Scheduling maintenance
• Determining lease charges
• Validating guarantees
• Setting customer charges
• Calculating costs per miles
• AND MORE

Guarnteed accuracy within + 2%

Stemco-Engler driveless hubodometers are specifically engineered to provide mileage accuracy. The fact is, we guarantee accuracy within + 2% for the life of the tyre. We know that lost miles mean lost revenues, so we've designed them to give you the most accurate readings possible.

Stemco-Engler's superior design

Independent mainshaft reduces failure caused by frontal impact.

Spring-loaded counterweight effectively reduces spin.

Externally pinioned odometer mechanism utilizes low friction moulded components.

AND THE WHEELS GO ROUND 1 - THE HUBODOMETER

The hubodometer has become a valuable aid in the operation of modern buses. In the 1950s and 1960s when a new route was to be tried the usual practice was for the Gaffer and a driver to go round in the former's car a couple of times, note the mileage and that gave a rough estimate of fuel consumption - typically 14 mpg on petrol or 20 on diesel. Nowadays competition is so cut-throat that the difference between a Dennis Dominator (Gardner engine) at 6.63 mpg, Leyland Olympian (Cummins) 6.92 mpg and Leyland Atlantean (Leyland) 8.82 mpg can make all the difference between profit and loss. Couple the easy availability of a mileage check given by a hubodometer with computer recorded and controlled fueling and a day to day check on fuel pricing, and exact cost is easily attainable.

Garlock (G.B.) Ltd.

A. Bristol with hubodometer

B. Leyland.

C. Guy.

D. A.E.C.

E. Bristol.

F. Bedford.

G. B.M.M.O.

H. Bristol.

I. Austin.

J. Daimler.

AND THE WHEELS GO ROUND 2 - AND ROUND

For effective Brushwork use

NULAC

The finish on your vehicles will look better and last longer if "Nulac" Coach Enamels and Varnishes are used. "Nulac" — the Master Finish — is specified by the Majority of Transport Undertakings in this country. Particulars from :-

ROBERT KEARSLEY & CO. · RIPON · YORKSHIRE

Robert Kearsley of Ripon were one of the very few companies involved in the PSV industry to treat the subject insofar as advertising was concerned in anything like a light-hearted manner. Certainly in early postwar years their artists, instead of extolling the range of colours produced (which reproduced awfully on the paper available) or trying to baffle would-be customers with technical spiel, chose to make a point obliquely. Incidentally, the vandalism shown was then a bad case of shock! horror! while today paint daubing on coaches parked up for the night is just another worry and expense. Ten years after this advert No. 173 of the Leicester City Transport was delivered from the bodybuilders, Metro-Cammell-Weymann. The PD3/1 chassis was usual enough and indeed LCT obtained 117 PDs in total, commencing May 1958 and terminating December 1967, although a further batch was on order, a purchase stultified by the Transport Act of 1968 which required all new vehicles to be suitable for one-person-operation. This objective was met by changing to front loading Leyland Atlanteans. So simply constructed were the PD3s that each only cost £6,504 per vehicle in 1967, whereas fifteen years later an Atlantean cost over ten times that amount. The style of MCW bodies on these vehicles has been described as "a monstrous mass of shivering tin", the superb paintwork, a credit to both manufacturers and workmen, does little to camouflage this effect. 173 was withdrawn in March 1975.

FIG. 1.

Showing Gear when door is closed.

Sample Sets can be supplied from Stock for trial purposes.

Owing to the positive locking an ascending handle may be fitted to the door for use when the door is open, without any risk of the door moving when the passenger pulls himself into the bus, consequently eliminating any risk of accident.

The gear occupies very little space as it allows the doors to fold almost to each other, thus allowing a wider actual entrance than is possible otherwise.

The device is both a locking arrangement (in both the open and shut positions) and also the most effective and quickest method of opening and closing doors. (The door can be moved from the locked shut position to the locked open position in one second, and vice-versa).

The gear is very simple to fit.   The gear is fool-proof.   Has only one moving part.

The door gear is also suitable for doors opening against the front bulkhead or any partition, the only difference is, instead of the lever handle being fixed, this is hinged to allow same to lie flush.

The gear has been fitted in buses supplied and on order to the following :—

Leeds Corporation	Ramsbottom U.D.C.	Mr. S. Ledgard, Leeds.
Doncaster Corporation	Grimsby Corporation	Williamson's Garage, Heanor.
Oldham Corporation	Gloucester Corporation	A. R. Graham, Ltd., Kirkintilloch.
Rotherham Corporation	Bury Corporation	Stevenson's Garage, Uttoxeter.
York Corporation	West Yorkshire Road Car Co.	Mr. H. G. Orr, Bolton.
West Hartlepool Corporation	Crossley Motors Ltd., Manchester.	

These fittings are made in best quality Admiralty Gun Metal and Mild Steel, Heavily Nickel Plated, or any other finish that may be required, or in Firths' Stainless Steel.

SOLE MANUFACTURERS:

GABRIEL & CO., LTD.,   4 and 5, A.B. ROW, BIRMINGHAM.

A loose door on any coach or bus is an unpleasant thing, being draughty, rattly and too often quite dangerous, and many have been the attempts to solve this problem. The most efficient involves the use of a sliding door, preferably operating between two skins (as favoured by Harringtons in the '30s) which actuated by a chain and counterweight always returns to the closed position. The worst was a manual folding door commonly found in 1950s underfloor engined vehicles which, at speed (30 mph!) gradually opened, leaving the driver to enjoy the flurries of snow or horizontal rain which blew in until such time as a brave passenger pushed it shut. (The alternative, to stop and do it oneself was not really on). Weird and wonderful mechanical devices were tried to reduce this difficulty, one in a 1956 body involved a lever placed adjacent to the gearlever on a manual gearbox AEC Reliance. The two knobs were alike in height and feel and they could be, and often were, confused. Opening the door when you are seeking second gear on a 1 in 9 hill is quite morale-lowering. Modified, the door mechanism never did work properly thereafter. This device of the 1920s was magnificently simple, foolproof and cheap, but one would guess after a year or two's misuse it would rattle and those woodscrews do look rather tishy.

Gabriel & Co.

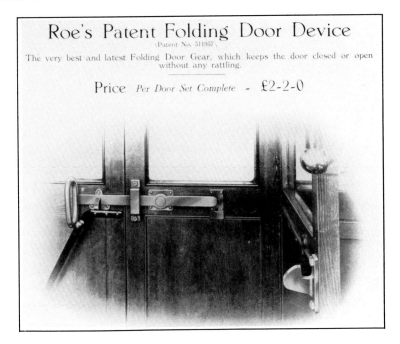

Roe's Patent Folding Door Device
(Patent No. 311957).

The very best and latest Folding Door Gear, which keeps the door closed or open without any rattling.

Price *Per Door Set Complete* - £2-2-0

Making it clear what PETERS build for buses!

2 SEATING

3 COMPRESSED AIR
   BRAKE

4 COMPRESSOR

5 "SUNDEALA" ROOFING

6 VENTILATOR

7 BLINDS

8 DOOR OPERATING
   MECHANISM

G. D. PETERS & CO., LTD., WINDSOR WORKS, SLOUGH, BUCKS

The versatility of a good manufacturer is nowhere more apparent than in this 1948 advertisement. Although items were still in very short supply and trading in export markets the main interest nonetheless one could order goods from a British firm confident they would be made in Britain by British labour.

Resistoid was one of a number of firms supplying handrails and similar fittings (Gabriel & Co. of A.B. Row, Birmingham was another that springs to mind) and it is logical for them to show a local vehicle, but one might add if the old Nor' Western Road Car brought their items it was a sign of confidence they would get quality work.   435, AJA 155, had a 1939 Gardner engined Bristol K chassis, rebuilt in 1951 with a new Willowbrook body as shown here.   She was withdrawn in 1965.

PRAY BE SEATED

Seating in buses and coaches must always represent a compromise between often almost irreconcilable requirements. The frame must be virtually indestructable, smooth, attractive in appearance but light. The covering material for bus seats must be hard wearing and easy to clean as, until recently at least, in industrial areas passengers upstairs usually wore greasy overalls or exuded brick, coal or plaster dust, from their clothing. And, not to mince words, lice and fleas were occasionally extra passengers even in the 1960s. Conversely when wooden seats were provided during the war these were most unpopular and very uncomfortable. Leather represents a good covering but was and is expensive, easily slashed and nowadays an easy target for 'Magic Marker' pens. A dull coloured moquette makes the vehicle uninviting but cheerful colours tend not to be entirely colourfast. Plastic and fibreglass seats are in anathema to any operator but here and there necessary in the vandal ridden 1990s. Yet the interior must attract for the passengers will only see the outside of a vehicle for, perhaps, ten minutes, whereas before the motorway age they could stare at the inside for ten hours with only short breaks. During the great days of coaching seats became almost volumptuous, lampshades took on the look of adjuncts to the new Odeon cinema, and veneers relieved the roof line. Individual mirrors attached to the back of seats were commonplace, ashtrays and cigarette stubbers obligatory, curtains of velvet repp added a cosy air, and the floor had to be carpeted.

But all this cost money, added weight and took up space, so that from the 1960s on the tendency has been to eliminate 'unnecessary' frills on all bar Executive-type coaches, although toilets, coffee machines, videos and air conditioning help to take away the boredom found by motorway age passengers.

Obviously seats appear here and there among the other photographs in this book, but whether we have progressed in passenger comfort between the 1920s and the 1990s is a matter of interpretation.

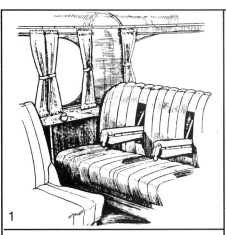

1

VARIATIONS UPON A COACH SEAT 1929

1. Arm-rests that fold up flush with the squabs
   divide the back row of the Hall, Lewis coach
   into four comfortable seats.

2. Moquette upholstered seats with cut-away
   arm-rests, made by Strachans.

3. Luxurious seat with high adjustable backs are
   a feature of the Metcalfe coach.

4. The type of armchair seat fitted by Duple
   Bodies to a Star coach.

5. Slightly staggered seats are a feature
   of the latest L.M.S. coach bodies. This body
   was built by Watson & Son, of Lowestoft.

2

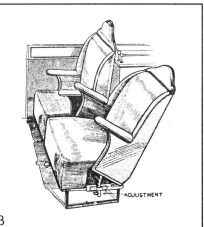

ADJUSTMENT

3

4

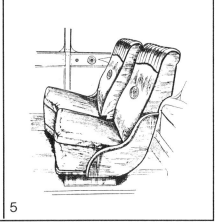

5

Strachan & Brown set up as coachbuilders during 1921 in Wales Farm Road, Acton and initially at least offered a bespoke service. Bus, coaches, commercial vehicles and even car bodies were all grist to their mill. Later "Strachans" and later still "Strachans Successors", their early vehicles showed some flair with unusual and often majestic designs - for example, coaches provided in 1928 for Aldershot & District which had a lean and fast look about them, while at the 1929 Commercial Vehicle Show an amazing modern-outline (for the time) 68 seat double-deck body was demonstrated. One of their 'trademarks' was the use of an oval rear window. The top photograph shows the contrast occasionally found between an extremely utilitarian floor and not very hardwearing seat covering while the lower shows both the bare ceilings, which streamed with condensation, yellowed from nicotine and were impossible to keep clean, and basic leather-covered seating. Both photographs date back to the mid-1920s.

SEATING OF THE LATE 1940s AND EARLY 1950s

1.　Described as having "artistic legs, with no castings to break", the detachable back, providing it did not involuntarily detach "allows repairs in Workshop without removal of frames". A price of £19. 13. 0 (£19.65) each ex-works included "Trimmed Moquette & Hide. Full headroll incorporating Hide Panels. Relief pipings. Repp on outer back and Chrome Recessed Ashtray".

2.　By contast, this semi-luxury seat was intended for "Service or Private Hire" (so-called All-Duty or Dual-Purpose) giving "Comfort with Economy in space" £14. 15. 0 (£14.75) each ex-works, trimmed in "Moquette with Hide Facings and Repp on Outer Back".

On 2 November 1932 Short Brothers (Rochester & Bedford) Ltd., of the Seaplane Works, Rochester completed this low-bridge forward entrance body on an AEC Regent chassis, supposedly for the Northern General Omnibus Company. Shorts had entered the coachbuilding field when the relatively sudden end of WW1 left them short of orders for seaplanes and indeed for a while part of the workshops was employed on household furniture building.

Here we are looking from the front entrance to the rear of the vehicle whose seats were upholstered in "premium quality furniture hide". The ceiling protrusion on the left is the well which forms the gangway beside the upstairs four-in-a-row seating. Unusually this does not carry the normal 'Mind your head' type warning which was quite vital, particularly for the occupants of the bench seat.

Notwithstanding the advances in chassis height reduction where low bridges were met the problem of how to obtain 'normal' centre aisle seating upstairs was to remain intractable until the arrival of the Lodekka and similar machines. The humped roof favoured in the late 1920s was one answer, another used not one but two side aisles, although of course this not only reduced capacity but probably caused twice as many bottom-deck heads to collide with the protrusions. The main snag of the four-in-a-row seat was the very slow loading and unloading as everyone had to move to let the 'inside' passenger out. At least one small boy anxious to get off was brusquely told to wait for the next stop as his young legs could walk back "and my old ones can't get used to this Jack-in-the-box game"; low height double deckers of the pattern shown here having recently replaced single deckers. Other points to note are the ankle-jarring steps to the forward row and the side emergency door (right hand side nearest the camera). The paucity of bell pushes with none on the 'inside' must have caused some chaos.

Two coach interiors deliberately chosen to show both the contrast and the improvement in thirty years. The older of the two is one of a batch of bodies built by Portsmouth Aviation (of The Airport, Portsmouth) who like many other companies in the military field found themselves short of work in the aftermath of war and, having a reasonable designer, probably lured from another company, sought to build bus and coach bodies. The driver remains relatively isolated in his cab next to the engine, and a canopy overhangs the vacant space on his left. Ventilation is by means of drop windows relying on friction grips. Opened they were draughty, closed they rattled. The obligatory mirrors and clock are fitted and as most services ran on time, given a copy of the timetable, the passenger knew when to get ready to disembark. Seating, individually numbered, is very comfortable and matching moquette is fitted to both the bulkhead and as a trim to the luggage rack. Polished wood fillets add a touch of class although the omission of curtains proves this is a day, rather than long distance, touring coach. Lighting, using tungsten lamps, give a warm glow, rather than a brilliant glare.

The Eastern Coach Works design has a curious bleakness about it compared with the earlier model, despite the carpeted floor and the contrasting colours and textures of the upholstery. By the time this design appeared the emphasis had swung over towards easier maintenance and a clean, Scandinavian look. The antimacassars, in either cotton or seersucker are both useful and if embroidered with the company name or initials a good advertisement, provided they are changed and cleaned regularly. Ventilation has greatly improved with 'ram air' scoops being fitted and fresh, filtered air is directed towards the passengers by individual controllable nozzles. Although nowhere near as good as air conditioning this system is relatively inexpensive and efficient when the vehicle is moving. The opening roof lights suggest a "belt and braces" attitude but are absolutely necessary when the vehicle is parked during the heat of the day. Individual reading lights supplement the dual day (white) and night (blue) tinted fluorescent tubes. Unfortunately these have an Achilles heel and a few hours with a tired tube flickering above the head can lead to queasiness or headaches. Magazine or map holders are fitted to the back of the seats which are semi-reclining when new, but often locked-up in later years as they can be a nuisance to the passenger behind. Like the Portsmouth Aviation body, ashtrays are fitted, an anathema to most passengers today. The engine has crept under the floor, so the driver shares the saloon with his passengers; his blind for nightdriving is the horizontal item apparently against the windscreen, but in reality located behind his seat.

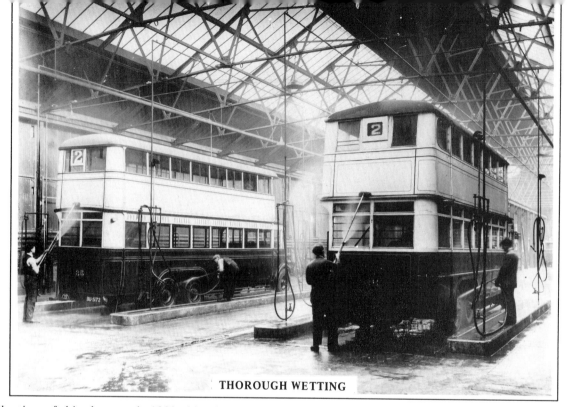

THOROUGH WETTING

At the time of this photograph, 1929, this vehicle wash plant in use by Oldham Corporation represented modernity. The hoses are certainly an advance on buckets, but whether the spray visible on the left hand side of No. 36 is intended or was merely a leak we shall never know. The total lack of protective gear for the men is noteworthy, but this was a semi-casual job insofar as the garage foreman selected his chosen men from the queue. No work, no pay.

No.35, BU 5172 is a 1928 Karrier WL6 built at Huddersfield, with English Electric 70 seat body work, its companion a Guy FCX, Wolverhampton built, also in 1928, its Roe body seating 72. Both were relatively short-lived, being gone before World War II, but were invaluable for shifting crowds of mill-workers four times a day, although from an engineer's viewpoint both makes were equally diabolical, suffering from poor initial design, lack of development and puny, fuel consuming (4 mpg!) engines whose lives were measured in weeks rather than months.

Eventually labour costs led to the development of automatic or semi-automatic wash plants, mostly out of doors as this model to be found at the rear of the bus garage belonging to Western National, Carvers Lane, Bridgwater, Somerset. Various designs exist, some automatically operated by a 'magic eye' others manually and in larger depots there may be a control cabin, originally often manned by a 'grounded' driver, who, although permanent night shifts were required, was glad enough to keep his rate of pay in any job. Modern washers often incorporate a water recycling device which can (if very sophisticated) extract the washing medium whether soap or mild acid. Some are quite ingenious being able in theory to wash fronts, backs and even roofs although often a black line or filthy half of the buses rear betrays the failure of the brush.

The ability of the traditional double decker to wade through floods is quite well known but rarely so graphically illustrated as in this photograph of a Guy Arab traversing The Square, Market Harborough, on 2 July 1958. June 1958 was one of the wettest on record in the area and the River Welland was already overflowing when heavy rain fell continuously during the 24 hours 9 a.m. 1 July to 9 a.m. 2 July. A total of 1.4" (36mm) in Market Harborough, North Kilworth 2.59" (66mm) and Hinckley 2.60" caused a further rise in the drains and tributaries feeding the Welland. Incidentally, the worst flood level recorded at this location in Harborough was between 7 and 8 feet (2.1 and 2.4m) deep, but this was in 1880. Subsequent river widening schemes between the town and Stamford are supposed to have eliminated any risk to future PSV services.

To <u>ALL MAINTENANCE STAFF</u>

From Depot Engineer

Subject Towing Wagon

Copies to Chargehands, File

Date 14 June 1984

Our reference KS/mgb N/t/s Your reference

Will All Maintenance Staff using Towing Wagon, Please
Ensure it is Kept Tidy, Water, Paper Towels, Diesel and Oil
If Used, are Topped up on Return To Garage.

K Snazle
Depot Engineer

Any fairly large coach company finds it necessary to own a service/breakdown vehicle. One or two find that this can become a self-financing operation as rescue work (particularly from motorways) can be undertaken for smaller companies. The problem there is, of course, that when you need the vehicle for one of your own buses in Kent, if may well be in Sussex!

The choice of base vehicle to use as a breakdown is governed by availability and the type of work envisaged, thus if double-deckers are liable to be a problem, an ex W.D. breakdown or heavy recovery vehicle is ideal, whereas if your requirement is for a dual recovery/stores vehicle then something nippy, perhaps redundant from your own fleet, is the obvious economic choice. The LC9 class of Leyland Leopards purchased by Midland Red in 1966 with Plaxton Panorama bodies had not been too successful as their limited seating (36) made them uneconomic to run in the 1970s. They were withdrawn between 1975 and 1976 and a number shortened and renumbered. After serving with Midland Fox No. 9000 (ex GHA 324D) was sold out of service in 1990 but is seen here in 1992 awaiting re-sale from her then owner.

INDEX TO THOSE MANUFACTURERS ILLUSTRATED